A Closer Look

DEDICATION

To anyone kind enough to tell me that what I do has pleased them.

Also to anyone who can convince me that what I do is as useful as real work.

Also to anyone who dislikes what I do yet has the kindness not to tell me so.

A Closer Look

WRITTEN AND ILLUSTRATED BY
Patrick Woodroffe

PRODUCED AND DESIGNED BY
Patrick Woodroffe

HARMONY BOOKS
New York

Published by Harmony Books, a division of Crown
Publishers, Inc., 225 Park Avenue South, New York,
New York 10003

HARMONY and colophon are trademarks of Crown
Publishers, Inc.

Manufactured in Singapore

Library of Congress Cataloging-in-Publication Data
Woodroffe, Patrick, 1940-
  A closer look.
  1. Woodroffe, Patrick, 1940-   —Sources.
2. Grotesque in art.   3. Art—Technique.   I. Title.
N6797.W66A35   1986   760′.092′4   86-19378
ISBN 0-517-56506-4

First Edition

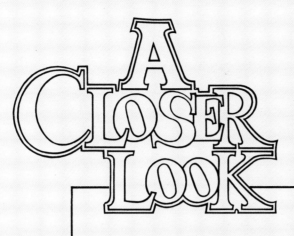

CONTENTS

SEA
SQUITLING

I have often thought that being an artist for a living is like spending the whole of your holiday writing postcards home. I feel such an urge to give some physical manifestation to my feelings and visions that I am sometimes perhaps in danger of missing out on the real reason for being alive.

Art is an extraordinary thing.

An artist embroiders real life by creating little fictions of his own. He uses these lies not only to amuse himself and to exorcise his deepest fears, but also to communicate with his fellows. It is his way of blurring the border-line between his own individual mental landscape and the external reality he believes he shares with others.

Yet surely the galleries are full, you may say — too full for comfort. Surely we have enough fiction already. Why make more? I don't know. Times change. We are all unique. Every man in history had a different pair of eyes. If even our finger-prints are never identical, then surely our visions must be infinitely varied. All our finger-prints, though different, are nonetheless recognizable as finger-prints, for we all have fingers. And our visions, though totally our own, must also be somehow familiar to every one of our fellow men, for we all have eyes.

Reality exists 'out there' — accepted by all, the stuff of our shared experience. Fiction exists only inside the brain — that is until some artist gives it form and substance. There will never be enough art, never enough fiction.

It's a magic thing, and strangely enduring. Once this fiction has been conjured up — even if it is only a child's fairy-tale — somehow it has a reality that can never be destroyed. There is a sense in which all fiction is truth.

BIOGRAPHY

1940 Born in Halifax, Yorkshire, England, son of an electrical engineer.

1964 Graduated in French and German at Leeds University.

1966 Small collection of pen and ink drawings ('Conflict') exhibited at the Institute of Contemporary Arts, London.

1972 Became a full-time painter, etcher and illustrator.

1972 Extended exhibition of paintings, etchings etc. at the Covent Garden Gallery, London.

1976 An exhibition of book-jacket and record-sleeve paintings at Mel Calman's 'Workshop' gallery, London.

1978 Approximately two hundred items on show at the historic Piece Hall in Halifax, Yorkshire.

1979 Complete illustrations for 'The Pentateuch' exhibited at the World Science-Fiction Convention, Metropole Hotel, Brighton.

1986 'Catching the Myth' — an exhibition selected from almost twenty years' work — Metropole Arts Centre, Folkestone.

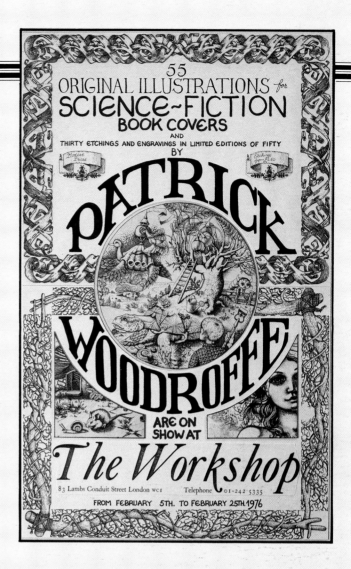

In the 1986 Folkestone show 'Catching the Myth' there were 122 exhibits.

This book covers a period of more than twenty years, a time in which not only my approach to painting — my reasons for doing it — but also my methods, have undergone radical changes.

I was not trained in fine art but in modern languages. I was a schoolmaster and a 'Sunday painter' for a good many years before leaving to become a full-time freelance artist. Painting offered me a seductive escape-route into a romantic world of my own. I could travel to places where no one else could go. I could invent my own world, furnish it with my own birds and beasts — even my own gods.

There were problems at the start of course — mostly financial — but I did eventually manage to make a living from painting, to get paid for enjoying myself immensely.

This is not a 'how to do it' book; it is a 'how I did it' book. It does not pretend to be a comprehensive technical guide. No doubt real artists — people trained at art schools, people who know what they are talking about — will tell you that much of the information in this book is not only out of date, but also out of touch with the methods and materials mainly in use today. I admit to being a little old-fashioned, a bit of an old woman in fact, obsessively tidy, painstakingly neat. I am certainly in no position to set myself up as any kind of authority, being taught only by reference books and bitter experience, but there are certain processes and tips which I am sure are completely my own and therefore worth passing on.

Anyway, I hope this book will succeed in conveying at least some useful information, and also — through the illustrations themselves — perhaps I may communicate something of my own vision of how things should be, so that this book, like all my others, may be seen to tell it not 'how it is' but 'how it could be'.

The children's book MICKY'S NEW HOME appeared in 1976 after much valuable help from Peter Jones of the Welsh Arts Council. It is a casebound quarto volume of 26 pages and contains twenty watercolour illustrations in full colour. Monochrome embellishments originated in etchings.

It was published in Welsh and English editions by D. Brown & Sons Ltd., Cowbridge, South Wales, and a German edition was later produced by Dragon's World in association with Sauerländer.

MYTHOPOEIKON (my own word — myth-making images) appeared in the same year. It is a comprehensive collection of approximately ten years' work, mainly in the field of book-jacket and record-sleeve illustration. There are 155 pages 297×210mm. . 145 of the illustrations are in full colour, forty in black and white. Once again it is decorated with monochrome cartouches and vignettes taken from etchings.

Mythopoeikon was published in English by Dragon's World and has also appeared in the Dutch language (in association with Becht) and in German (Moewig).

THE ADVENTURES OF TINKER THE HOLE-EATING DUCK (Dragon's World/Paper Tiger) took exactly one year to produce, but was not published until 1979. It is also in the A4 format, and has 46 pages. 32 of the illustrations are in full colour, 34 in black and white. As before, the design includes monochrome embellishments.

The book was translated into Dutch and published in association with Spectrum. It also came out in Germany with Sauerländer.

THE PENTATEUCH OF THE COS-MOGONY sold 50,000 copies between 1979 and 1984. Published by Dragon's World in association with EMI Records, it is a collaboration with symphonic rock composer Dave Greenslade. Two long-playing records of Greenslade's music are packed with a casebound 47 page book measuring 305 × 305mm.. There are 59 illustrations in full colour, 8 in black and white. It purports to be the first five chapters of an alien Book of Genesis, and is sub-titled 'The Birth & Death of a World'.

The foreground illustration shown here was not in the end used for the cover. The more hard-selling desert landscape (and shortened title) was considered more appropriate.

HALLELUJAH ANYWAY (Paper Tiger 1984) was originally intended as a follow-up to 'The Pentateuch' — another musical collaboration — but so far this has proved impossible to set up. It consists of a 136-page collection of illustrated lyrics. It is printed in full colour and measures 260 × 280mm. . There are 152 colour pictures and 8 in black and white.

This was the first time my 'tomographs' (painted cut-outs) appeared in print.

ONE: DRAWING

Pencil, pen & ink, Rapidograph, silverpoint, line & wash, tinting etc..

We draw with a solid stylus or crayon: we paint with a brush. That would seem to be the simple distinction, but it is difficult to define accurately the frontiers of each territory. At what point for example does a re-worked sketch become a drawing? When does a tinted drawing suddenly become a painting?

It may be fruitless to discuss it at all, but the use of these different terms sometimes betrays a rather perverse value judgement.

The painting — especially in oils — is widely regarded as the highest attainment of two-dimensional art, whereas sketches and drawings — I suspect because they usually involve less time and effort — are generally considered somewhat inferior. I don't understand this view; it frustrates me. I think rough sketches can often be more interesting than paintings. They are more spontaneous, more genuine. The original idea remains undegraded by indirect procedures.

Sketches and drawings also tend to be rated rather low if done for some literary or illustrative purpose. It seems they step too close to that dreaded frontier where 'fine art' becomes 'commercial art'. Illustrators such as Arthur Rackham and William Heath Robinson produced work of astounding quality, but I am sure it will be many years before their 'coloured drawings' or 'cartoons' command the high prices fetched at auction by more 'painterly' works — of the impressionists for example.

Until quite recently I regarded my own sketches merely as a preparation for later work to be done on a different surface entirely. To be honest I was rather ashamed of them. As pieces of 'art' they were awful, usually put away in a drawer and forgotten. But since then my roughs have got much better, and I have even been able to ink them up and tint them in such a way that they can be seen as finished oil-paintings, without (I hope) spoiling the spontaneity of the first idea.

The character of any drawing is undoubtedly dictated by the methods and materials used. There is no way for example, that vigorous and spontaneous sketching can be done with a 9H pencil or a silverpoint stylus. The reason is purely mechanical. A hard, sharp point rubbed on a hard, unyielding board can only produce a stiff, 'tight' result, with few carefree

Below: *Very accurate and precise pencil drawing is possible only when pencils and papers are comparatively hard. I prefer a long tapering point, for this can be re-sharpened many times on an abrasive block before I need to cut it again.*

Short pencil-ends can still be used in a 'porte-crayon'; mine is home-made — a piece of dowel drilled at one end.

By resting the drawing hand on a piece of scrap paper, the work is protected from grease.

Above and opposite: *This pen and ink drawing (THE LONG LIE-IN 1983) began as a pencil sketch on cheap scrap paper. It was never intended to become finished work, but was to be traced onto primed hardboard and completed in oils. But lack of time forced me to use a quicker and more spontaneous method.*

The cheap paper was mounted on board and the drawing completed in ink. Tinting with mainly transparent oils meant that very little was lost of the vigour of the original sketch.

flourishes and no scribbles. It is necessarily and visibly the product of pains-taking effort.

A 2B graphite pencil on the other hand, can give an obviously more relaxed effect, soft and dark areas achieved with a minimum of hard work.

Extremes of technique have their different merits. They are not mutually exclusive. The choice of tools should be dictated only by the job to be done, and interesting effects can often be accomplished by combining very different techniques in one piece of work.

For accurate and detailed pencil drawing it is obviously best to use hard pencils (HB to 5H) on a very smooth surface. For this kind of work I use Daler 'Truline' or illustration board. This not only has a fairly yielding surface, which makes the job more relaxed, but it is also a firm and hard-wearing support, which means that the work can be frequently corrected with a rubber.

I find it difficult to start work, especially on something new, but it helps me if I observe one or two careful rituals. I am quite sure that this sort of approach would not suit everyone, but I have found that I need to encourage a particular state of mind before I begin.

One of these rituals concerns my pencils. I have nothing against modern .5 millimetre propelling pencils — I use them all the time for sketching, because they never need sharpening — but for very fine work you can't beat the old-fashioned wooden pencil. I always have a stock of ready-sharpened pencils. Not only is this a good morale-booster at the start of a day's work, but it also means that I don't have to stop working just when things are going well. I cut a very long tapering point — for two reasons. A tapering point can be easily re-sharpened many times on an abrasive block before needing cutting again. It may also be used at a low angle for delicate shading work, which — if the pencil is periodically twisted — will also keep the point needle-sharp for accurate details.

Another little ceremony I observe is to place my drawing hand on a piece of scrap paper or cloth to protect the work from grease. This is specially important if any tinting is to be done later; washes do not take easily on greasy surfaces.

A good sharp rubber is also needed. I always buy a big one and cut it up into thin slices so that I can make very tiny erasures. It is a good idea not to cut slices until you need them, as the rubber inevitably deteriorates when exposed.

Although extremely fine and accurate drawing can be done with a sharp graphite pencil, a silverpoint can achieve almost microscopic detail.

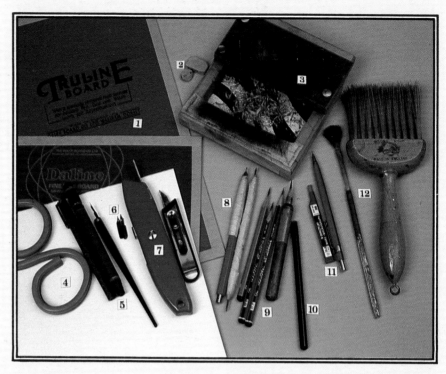

Above: *Good quality prepared boards (1) are the best surface for precise pencil drawing. Rubbers go a long way when cut into thin slices (2). An abrasive block made from fine 'wet & dry' (3) is especially useful if it is mounted on a small box which can catch not only the graphite dust but also pencil shavings. The small piece of rag along the edge is for wiping fine dust off the pencil point. A flexible French curve (4) is rarely useful except in extremely tight Rapidograph drawing. In fact most drawing aids are better avoided. The Rapidograph pen (5) is a wonderfully accurate instrument, but will not make a spontaneous drawing unless old and malfunctioning. However, it is very useful for making fine adjustments to conventional pen drawings. The traditional steel dip-pen (6) is undoubtedly one of the most vigorous and expressive of all drawing instruments. It is not for the timid. For pencil-sharpening I prefer a heavy duty DIY knife (7); it is fairly easy to make a long tapering point. An old clutch pencil (8) is a useful*

holder for silver wire in silverpoint drawing. Copper wire may be used in the same way, but is not so reliable for drawing; it does however make a good tracing stylus. Different grades of pencil (9) are used for different purposes. I use most of the range from 6B to 9H. A graphite stick (10) with a chisel point is an excellent tool for rough expansive sketching. A fine (.5mm.) propelling pencil (11), especially with soft leads (2B), is probably the most useful tool when accuracy and spontaneity are of equal importance. Dusting brushes (12) are useful for removing rubbings from the work without smudging or greasing it up. Mine really need a good wash.

Opposite page: *Sketch THE BILLIARD CUE MARKER (1983) for the project 'The Hunting of the Snark'.*

Using a .5mm. (2B) propelling pencil, sketching can proceed with great accuracy as well as freedom.

A properly made silverpoint stylus can be bought from an art supplier, but I have always used either bits of silver cut from old jewellery or silver wire bought from a silversmith's workshop. The latter can be conveniently used in place of a lead in a modern clutch pencil. Sharpening is done on the abrasive block.

Incidentally, a clutch pencil barrel is also a convenient holder for sharpened copper wire to be used as a stylus for tracing.

The difficulty with silverpoint is to get a satisfactory white ground on which to work, for neither paper nor board give results without careful preparation. I have used several types of acrylic and glue-based grounds for this, but success has never been predictable. The chemical properties of pigments and binders are so diverse that it is difficult to pass on a recipe, but I have had good results with a fairly weak solution of Scotch glue mixed with titanium white powder pigment. It may be that this mixture suits only the type of silver I have been using, so it is probably advisable for a beginner to buy all the materials — including properly prepared boards — from a good supplier such as Cornelissen of London.

Silverpoint is a very anxious and demanding technique in which corrections are virtually impossible without scraping away and retouching the white ground. Not only that — rough preparatory sketching is practically impossible as well, even with a soft pencil.

My method is to do a fairly minimal, though accurate pencil sketch *before* laying the ground. If the ground is thin enough, the sketch will be visible through it, though there is an obvious danger that the ground will tend to scrape away easily if there is a great deal of glossy graphite underneath it.

With debatable success I have also experimented with silverpoint in conjunction with watercolour and acrylic gouache. The gouache ground is waterproof, which means that transparent glazes of watercolour can be applied on top to give touches of high colour. Alternatively the ground itself may have small amounts of colour mixed with it before it is laid.

However, silverpoint has such a subtle delicacy that it shows up rather badly on a coloured ground. The austere purity of the medium is unique, and although it contrasts very well in close proximity with highly coloured areas, it is most effective on its own or in very low-key combinations.

Having read that virtually any metal might be used as a drawing stylus, I have experimented — though only once — with copper. I used the same ground as for silverpoint, but unfortunately some obscure chemical

THREE SHELLS FRUIT-JUICE ANALOGUE (1978) This drawing from 'The Pentateuch' combines many media. Watercolour, airbrush and gold ink seem to enhance the soft austerity of the silverpoint panel in the centre. Silver will produce extremely accurate lines, and although the amount of contrast is limited, this gentle greyness is part of its charm. (The detail below is enlarged to approximately twice actual size).

Silverpoint seems most effective when used with other monochrome media. In this close-up from FOR ENGLAND AND SAINT GEORGE! (1981) only the middle section is in silverpoint. The sky was previously air-brushed in ink, the sleeping dragon was drawn with Rapidograph and steel pens, and everything else was drawn with a brush and dilute waterproof ink. Only in the silverpoint area was the Truline board given a ground of titanium white. (Detail slightly enlarged).

Above: *For POOR OLD GEORGE (1980) a glue/titanium white ground was laid over a pencil sketch on Truline board. The sketch was visible enough to be a guide for the copperpoint work which followed. Fortunately I photographed the drawing immediately, for within a week all the copperpoint work had faded away to nothing. So far the prophecies of experts — that it may one day return in strength — remain unfulfilled! (Detail slightly enlarged).*

Above:
This drawing for 'The Pentateuch' (1978) has also presented problems. The malicious Ildrinn (executed in silverpoint, inks, watercolour etc.) today remains as strong as ever, but poor old God (drawn almost entirely in copperpoint) has all but faded away. It is reproduced here from a transparency taken when the drawing was new.
(Reduced to approximately half actual size.)

18

Above:
*This playing-card motif for 'The Pentateuch',
THE BEGINNING & THE END (1979)
combines not only silverpoint, watercolour, air-brush
etc., but also etching. Before any other work was started,
the central panel was embossed by passing the Truline
board through the press with a small uninked etched
plate. (Approximately actual size.)*

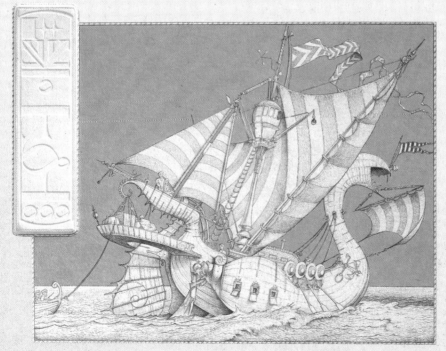

Left:
*In this vignette for 'The Pentateuch' (1978), the
silverpoint foreground is set off by a blue sky in gouache
(opaque watercolour). The ideogram title was embossed
from an etched plate. For some reason silverpoint seems
at its best in subtle monochrome combinations or on its
own. (Slightly reduced.)*

reaction took place, and several days' work simply vanished within a week. Luckily I had already photographed the drawing, and I have been told by an expert that it could well reappear one day. Meanwhile, I keep it in a drawer and wait. Not surprisingly, that experience has so far made it easy for me to resist the temptation to experiment with other metals.

Much graphic work for reproduction has to be 'line', that is black and white with nothing in between. Here all the subtleties of pencil and silverpoint must give way to the starkness of pen and ink, where all half-tone effects have to be made up in various ways with lines and dots.

The most revolutionary development in this field has been the introduction of the Rapidograph, a fountain-pen with a tubular nib which is capable of extraordinary control and accuracy. It is an essential tool for producing ruled lines or stipples where uniformity and precision are more important than expression and spontaneity. The Rapidograph should be used sparingly, for if a drawing is produced entirely by using one Rapidograph or only one width of nib, the result — although extremely controlled and sharp — will certainly lack vigour and contrast.

This problem can be overcome simply by combining the Rapidograph with other tools, notably the ordinary steel dip-pen, whose springing, resilient nib can produce a highly expressive line of varying width.

The most effective line illustrations of all — those of Dürer or Schongauer for example — come from engravings on copper or wood, techniques where the swelling line is an unavoidable part of the process. A steel pen can to some extent imitate this swelling line, though with much greater freedom and vigour. It is an extremely effective tool for transforming a sketch into line art-work. Small touches of ink may be put in very tentatively at first, then built up by more confident, heavier strokes as the drawing becomes established. Large areas of black can be filled in with a sable brush, and small adjustments and stipplings may be added very accurately with the Rapidograph after the main drawing has been completed.

Opaque white gouache may also be used if the drawing is intended merely as artwork for reproduction. Small touches can be put in here and there to correct and improve edges, to sharpen corners etc..

When producing line artwork for lettering etc., I generally make drawings at least twice as large as the size at which they are to appear in print. This makes it easier to make fine corrections and improvements either in black or white. Over-correction is however best avoided, for it is rather

Although the Rapidograph is an excellent tool for precise graphic work, it is best used in conjunction with a steel dip-pen if an over-mechanical effect is to be avoided.

In these pages from 'The Adventures of Tinker the Hole-Eating Duck' (1976) most of the structural lines were put in first with a steel pen, and the rapidograph was used mainly as a stippling tool.

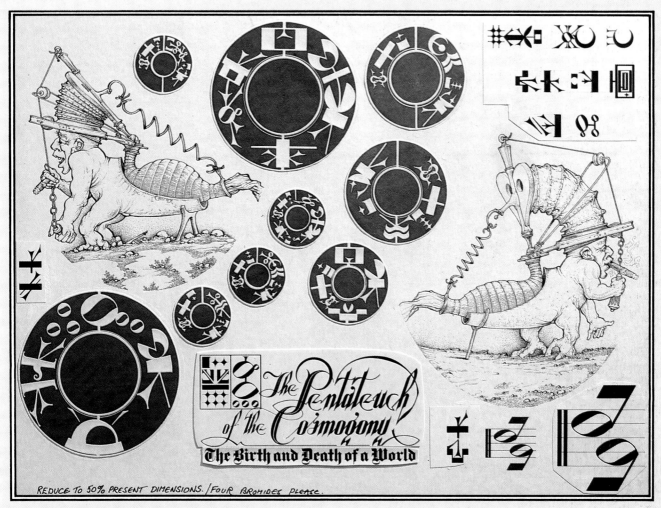

REDUCE TO 50% PRESENT DIMENSIONS. / FOUR BROMIDES PLEASE.

Above: Line artwork for reduction ('The Pentateuch' 1979) can be made in many ways. This assemblage was prepared so that small additions and embellishments could be added to the 'paste-up' text.

The two cigar-puffing 'pollutocrats' were drawn with steel and Rapidograph pens on the Truline board itself. The discs of ideograms are surface prints from etched plates produced for another purpose. The titling is already a bromide reduction of a much larger drawing. The small symbols were drawn very precisely on plastic sheet before they were stuck down here to be photographed.

Below:
The Rapidograph really comes into its own when used to make precise modifications to work done mainly with a traditional steel dip-pen.

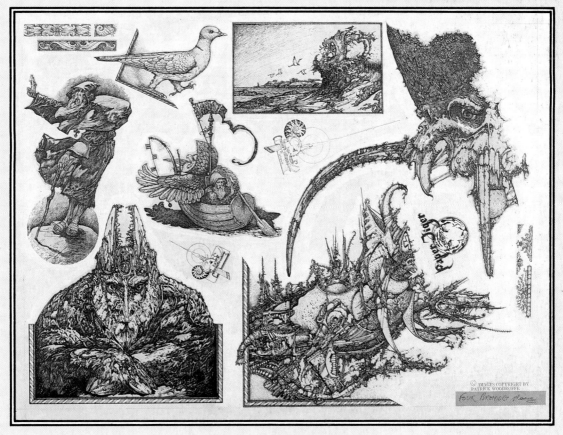

21

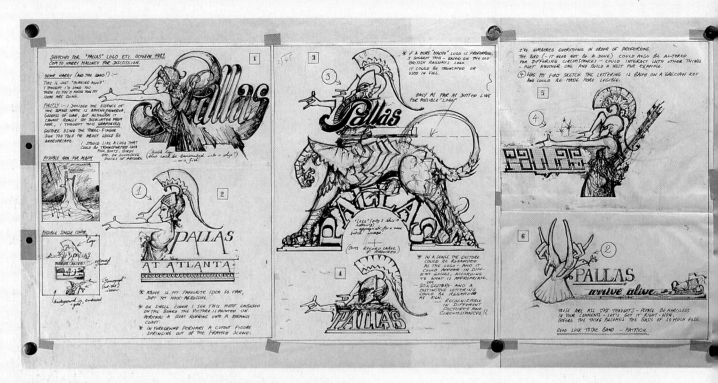

Above: Pen and ink can be a very effective sketching medium, especially when the end result is to be used as line artwork for reproduction. These sketches show the progression of my ideas when I was asked to design a logo for the rock-band PALLAS in 1983.

Using the three-fingered salute which is one of their stage gestures, I began by thinking only of Pallas Athena, the goddess of war. The gesture of loosing a non-existent arrow from a non-existent bow became a potent symbol of dynamic pacifism. The figure eventually became male, armoured, a mechanical centaur, victim of a polluted and callous technological nightmare. He leaps across the 'Sentinel' album in pursuit of doves. The hunt is a charade, for the hunter has no weapon. The doves — like fans at a concert — need only mimic his gesture with their wings to become invulnerable, enclosed with him in a dynamic vortex of sound.

The finished line artwork was used not only to make reductions for the paste-up, but also to provide a basis for letterheads, logotypes and a mass of merchandising and ancillary uses. Posters, badges, T-shirts — even costumes for the band and a uniform for the roadies — emerged from these humble drawings.

22

The Pallas centaur appeared not only on the album cover but also on subsequent singles and on their recent 12" release 'The Knightmoves'.

The top copy of the album is shown open at the gatefold. This was signed for me by all the members of the band. The text was written out on tracing paper placed over a lined grid; it then had to be twice reduced in order to accommodate all the lyrics in the spread.

The 'bag' for the single 'Shock Treatment' opened up as a poster showing an image also used in my book 'Hallelujah Anyway' (THE WERHOB-MAGOG).

The album was also sold with free posters, and some singles were produced as picture-discs.

difficult and risky to add further black work on top of white corrections.

Working on a larger scale also makes it possible to use drawing aids such as stencils, ruler, compasses etc. . A flexible French curve can be useful when flowing lines need to be extremely accurate — in decorative titling for example — though I should never use one for any other purpose as they tend to ossify the expressive line.

Perhaps it is somewhere here, in the choice of equipment and drawing aids, that the real borderline exists between art and graphics. There are times when drawing machines, templates and stencils are essential, but quite often their use can destroy and de-humanize otherwise good work.

Methods of making line artwork for reproduction are changing all the time. The artwork is usually reproduced from 'bromides' (photographic prints), which are then 'pasted up' onto boards with the text etc. . Because the method is photographic, work may be reduced, then worked on again or used in conjunction with work that has not been reduced. I have achieved quite interesting results by using ordinary Xerox reductions — re-worked, corrected and adjusted — on paste-ups. Though not so accurate, these reductions do have the advantage of being much cheaper than bromides.

A good method of obtaining quick line artwork is in fact to have a strong Xerox copy made of a pencil drawing, then to add details later with a pen or Rapidograph. This saves a lot of effort with the steel pen, but cannot be regarded as safe or permanent work.

Where the steel pen really comes into its own is as a sketching-tool for producing free and expressive drawing over pencil. It is a good way for example of making preparatory sketches for etchings, though it must always be remembered that the technique of etching can never imitate the spontaneity of a pen and ink sketch. In fact it is generally bad practice to develop ideas in one technique, intending to reproduce them slavishly as finished work in another.

To produce colour work from pen drawings, it is possible to tint over waterproof inks with watercolour washes. Alternatively, non-waterproof inks can be used for the drawing, so that lines may be adjusted and softened during the tinting process. The greatest master of the pen drawing must surely be Arthur Rackham, who — using a similar technique — managed to preserve the vigour of a sketch in finished colour illustrations of great subtlety and detail.

My own technique is to re-work a sketch in pen and ink, and then to tint it with transparent oil-paints. In this

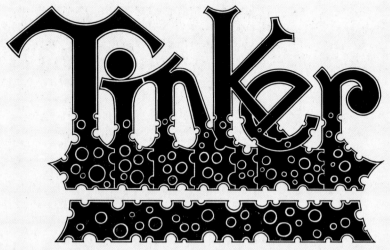

Above: *The titling which appears on the English edition of 'The Adventures of Tinker the Hole-Eating Duck' (1976) was designed by Roger Dean. My own titling shown here was done with a Rapidograph and a sable brush and black ink. This was one of the many titling ideas I had for this book, none of which were used in the end.*

Please note that all the holes have been eaten. (Approximately half original size).

Below: *The Rapidograph is a wonderful tool for precise geometric work. The 'mystic rose' figure is* achieved simply by joining each equally-spaced point on a circle to every one of its fellows. The extraordinary concentric patterns so produced are very beautiful and particularly baffling when repeated as an ellipse. The second ellipse shown here is also in perspective, and the vortex pattern derived from it was used in my illustration for the cover of 'In the Kingdom of the Beasts' (Stableford — see 'Mythopoeikon' p.79).

The chequered Archimedes spiral was done purely as an experiment, but it came in handy for the cover of 'The Door into Summer' (Heinlein — see 'Mythopoeikon' p.106).

Titling for 'The Pentateuch' (1979) presented many problems. The word itself is not commonly used, so it needed to be fairly legible. This limited the opportunity for excessive embellishment. Much of the work was done using my drafting table, but curved parallel lines of this precision were only possible with the aid of a flexible French curve. A .5mm. rapidograph pen was used for much of the work, though large areas were filled in with a brush. The original drawing was approximately twice the size shown here.

The Pentateuch

Dave Greenslade

Below:
When I produced the black and white titling for 'Micky's New Home' way back in the early seventies, I was new to book production and took the unnecessary trouble of drawing out the titling several times larger than the printed size and in four languages, only to find later that the fount was readily available in Letraset, and that the job could have been done in a matter of hours rather than days — and with much greater accuracy.

CARTRE
NEWYDD
MICI

Ysgrifennwyd ac arluniwyd gan

Patrick Woodroffe

Patrick Woodroffe

· CATCHING · THE · MYTH ·

· AN · EXHIBITION · OF · FANTASY ·

PAINTINGS, ETCHINGS, DRAWINGS, TOMOGRAPHS & WORDS

12th OCTOBER ~ 10th NOVEMBER
Monday to Saturday 10~5, *Sunday* 2.30~5

PATRICK WOODROFFE
will talk about
"The Way I Work"
WEDNESDAY 23RD OCTOBER IN THE GALLERY AT 7.30 P.M.
(*Admission* £1.50.)

ARTS CENTRE *at the* 'MET'
Metropole Arts Centre
The Leas Folkestone
Tel: 0303 55070

Grant Aided by South-East Arts Association

KENT LITERATURE Festival

15th ~ 20th October 1985.

Left:

    This paste-up for my recent show in Folkestone is made up from various separate elements. The titling was that used for 'The Pentateuch' (1979); this is a bromide from the same batch. The central drawing is a Xerox of a pencil sketch, subsequently fortified and adjusted with Rapidograph and white gouache.

    The two logotypes, which were added later by gallery staff, are apparently part of a letter-heading and a self-adhesive promotional sticker.

Right:

    To produce sufficiently authentic bureaucratic touches in the introductory passage for 'The Pentateuch' (1979) I had various rubber stamps made from my own line artwork.

    'Project Hermes' was the scientific investigation of an alien 'Marie Celeste' which had orbited Saturn for thousands of years but was not discovered until the year 2378.

    The UNTW logotype, incorporating only the essential parts of a pyramid of ten interlocking circles, represents the 'United Nations of the Ten Worlds'.

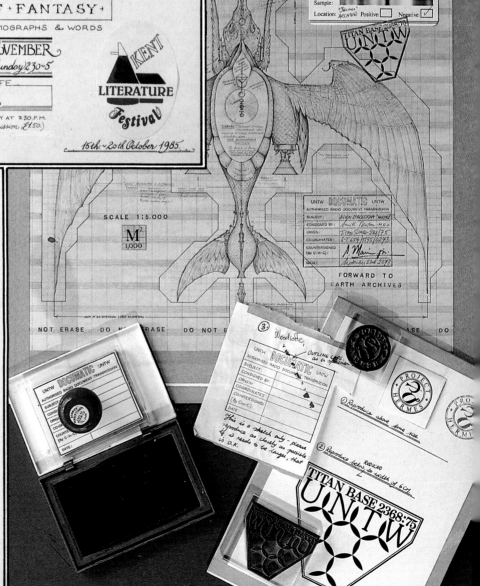

Above: *In this pen and ink sketch for the subsequent etching* THE RUNAWAY BULL *(1985), most of the work was done with a traditional steel dip-pen. The paper is only cheap computer print-out stock, but this has a considerable advantage over thicker papers for this purpose in that it can be traced through very easily. If a copper stylus is used, the drawing is unaffected by the tracing process.*

The portion between the irate farmer and the bull itself was inserted later, when I decided to alter the shape of the etching plate. Later, after tracing, the whole drawing was carefully mounted on hardboard using dilute wood-working adhesive (white resin).

The motto which eventually accompanied this etching ran as follows:

'The smoke from the fire just flies away
 The tide leaks through to the narrow bay;
 If you read the assassin's false pretence
 Get you gone to a field that has no fence.'
(The etching is shown on pages 50 and 51.)

Below: *A similar procedure was used for the companion etching* THE PROUD FATHER *(1985), but in this case the preliminary sketch turned out to be on too small a piece of paper. The area containing the bull and the calf is a slightly different colour from the L-shaped area containing most of the tree and foliage.*

The motto eventually appearing with this etching was:

'If only the year would stay its clock
 In the term when the farmer spares his stock
 When even the mightiest cleaves to the meak
 And even a dumb beast's tongue may speak.'
(The etching is shown on pages 52 and 53.)

These sketches for a pair of etchings CHANGING PLACES (1985), were done mainly with a steel pen, though there is also much pencil work and some ink wash applied with a brush. The long tail of the 'magmoo' on the right (above) will of course be omitted from the etching, which will be in the same format as the companion piece below. This pair of etchings is intended as a sequel or extension of the more conventional imagery in the pair of sketches shown on the previous page.

'Ask not to change your given place
To trade your plumage or your face,
For when such change becomes contagious,
The consequence can prove outrageous!'

'If things could be the things they aren't   And get the things they think they want,   They'd still be bored with what they'd got

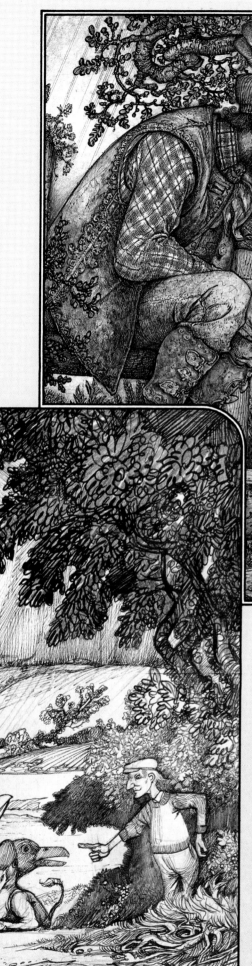

way many of my full-colour illustrations began as rough pencil sketches on humble computer print-out paper. However the paper could not have withstood the pen and ink — let alone oil-tinting — without first being mounted on hardboard.

To do this I first spray the sketch with fixative. When this has completely evaporated, I dampen the back of the paper with a large household paintbrush or sponge and place it carefully in position on the hardboard. I then fold forward the top half of the sketch and brush dilute woodworking adhesive (white resin) onto the hardboard. This means I can apply the adhesive without damaging or even displacing the damp sketch. I then lay the top down again, carefully push out any bubbles by rubbing my hand over another piece of paper placed over the sketch, then repeat the process with the lower half. It is an easy and almost infallible method of sticking down delicate items permanently without bubbles or creases. I have even mounted very large posters and sketches in this way. The hardboard should preferably be braced at the back with a wooden frame, otherwise the shrinking of the drying paper will distort it, but on small pieces this is not necessary.

After mounting, the sketch must be left to dry thoroughly before any pen and ink work is done, otherwise it will easily be scratched by the nib.

When all pen-work has been finished, the drawing is given several priming coats of Liquin (Winsor & Newton's oil/resin painting medium), which effectively isolates the paper from all subsequent work to be done in oils. The surface has a glassy smoothness and must be kept clean and free of grease. Touching it with the fingers may prevent the paint from taking properly.

Using mainly transparent glazes of oil-paints with Liquin medium, a very controllable tinting procedure is possible. Any mistakes can be literally wiped away with a rag. The transparency of the glazes gives the colour its greatest possible luminosity and strength, achieving many effects impossible in any other way.

Small highlights of opaque oil-colour may also be added, though this is best done sparingly. If too much opaque colour is used or if the lines are obscured by paint, then the drawing may trespass uncomfortably on the threshold of being a painting.

Very soft brushes must be used for this technique. Short-handled sable or synthetic brushes supplied for water-colour painting are best.

Another area where drawing comes very close to painting is in ink line and wash, especially if this involves using the full range of tones. Dilute waterproof inks are extremely effective if applied sparingly with a

In this detail from THE BAILIFF (1979) mainly transparent glazes of oil-paint have been applied over a pen and ink drawing. The original sketch — in pencil on computer print-out paper — was first mounted on board. Its spontaneity seems unimpaired by re-working in ink and colour, probably because no indirect techniques, involving tracing etc., have been used. (Very slightly reduced detail).

And changing places quite a lot.'

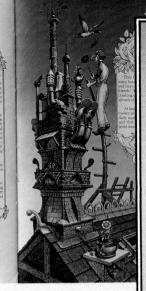

In this monochrome illustration for 'The Adventures of Tinker the Hole-Eating Duck' dilute waterproof Indian ink has been applied with very fine sable brushes. Small touches of white gouache have been added here and there for highlights.

The background was air-brushed while the foreground was protected by masking fluid. Later, when the brickwork was complete, the distorted rails in the foreground were again masked out so that the mist could be applied with the air-brush.
(Slightly enlarged detail).

In this illustration for 'Tinker', DING DONG: A NEW TOY FOR THE FISHES! the main lines were drawn with a steel pen. Details were added in very dilute ink with broad and fine sable brushes.

For parts of the background a Rapidograph was also used to apply very dilute ink.
(Detail slightly reduced).

·PALLAS MOVE·THE BLACK KNIGHT·

10

After the first Pallas album 'The Sentinel' I was asked to further explore the possibilities of the logo and produced another series of sketches.

Following a period of intensive sketching work on Mike Batt's project 'The Hunting of the Snark' (a musical based on Lewis Carroll's nonsense poem), I seemed to have developed a new, more dynamic sketching style which owed its character to the use of a .5mm. (2B) propelling pencil. This invaluable tool enables sketching

work to be both vigorous and precise.

The symbolism has come a long way since my original gentle Pallas Athena. The conflict, which before was only a game, now seems real, vicious, bestial, ultimately despairing. The Pallas beast is no longer a centaur; he is now a pawn in someone else's game; or is he a great dictator, or perhaps a sad old musician bewailing his lonely demise?

7   8

FLUTE SOLO AT THE WORLD'S END~

SERMON: CONDUCTOR OF THE UNHOLY CHOIR: ABOMINATION OF DESOLATION: THE BEAST

brush in the manner of watercolour. The difference comes from the fact that waterproof marks made with such inks can be repeatedly re-worked, building up effects which are impossible in watercolour. The use of masking fluid, which I shall describe later, is extremely easy and effective in this technique; the pigment is so delicate and weak that the dried film of masking fluid is particularly easy to remove.

Ink line and wash is undoubtedly best in monochrome or with only minimal colour. The sable brush may be the only tool, or it may be used in conjunction with the Rapidograph or steel pen, with silverpoint, air-brush etc.. A second Rapidograph may also be filled with very dilute ink to give a pale grey line rather than a black one. Subtle differences between varied techniques can give monochrome work an appealing, understated purity which is often more pleasing than work in full colour.

A basic principle becomes evident over and over again, whatever technique is used — the original character of a sketch or preliminary drawing should not be lost. A good sketch can have a quality of raw spontaneity and freshness that is as far from a painting or an etching as a rock-song is from a string quartet. They are not mutually exclusive; each is a valid genre, appropriate for the delivering of different messages.

I am very pleased with some of the sketches I have produced for various recent projects. I did a great deal of sketching work for example during my involvement with Pallas, a rock-band from Aberdeen, whose album 'The Sentinel' was copiously illustrated with my work. Tight deadlines meant that this first album cover had to be produced as a one-coat oil-painting, with no time either for sketching or underpainting, so when I was asked to continue working with them, I decided to get some preparation done well in advance.

It was interesting to explore the band's own symbolism in as many ways as I could, and to do this I had to work very fast. This is why I chose to use a .5 millimetre 2B propelling pencil — the ideal sketching tool. Not only does it never need sharpening, but if the pencil is periodically rotated in the hand, it always has a fine point which will make both very tentative marks and strong vigorous strokes.

A vigorous approach to sketching, not only for Pallas, but also in connection with Mike Batt's recent project 'The Hunting of the Snark', has taught me a lot about the function of line and tone in drawing. Not only that, I feel it has given me a greater understanding of the part played by line in the landscape and in Nature. There is a pervasive harmony in all forms as we see them, in rocks, skies,

Opposite page: *Details of four examples when preliminary sketches eventually turned out to be the basis of finished oil-paintings ('Hallelujah Anyway' 1984).*

The original sketches were in pencil. After proper mounting on hardboard, the sketches were re-worked in ink, and still later — after two coats of Liquin had thoroughly dried — they were tinted very thinly with mainly transparent glazes of oil-paint.

The method not only preserves the spontaneity of the original idea, but also allows black pen and ink to be coloured without loss of contrast. On the contrary, the layers of Liquin tend to enrich the black of the ink. (Variously slightly reduced details.)

Above: *In this detail from FOR ENGLAND AND SAINT GEORGE (1981), and in the two little vignettes (below) from 'Tinker' (1978), very pale tones and gradations are achieved with extremely dilute waterproof ink applied with a fairly large pointed sable (No.3). Very fine detail and black line work is done both with a steel pen and with very fine (000) sable brushes.*

foliage etc., which has a great deal to do with half-hidden spirals, turbulences, concentricities and parallels — all distorted, foreshortened and variously truncated by our human vantage-point at almost ground level.

Without at least a partial understanding of how these rhythmic currents operate, it is difficult to make convincing line-drawings of landscapes and creatures, and whereas a line can point out and emphasize these currents, a wholly tonal drawing remains somehow motionless, strangely flat and dead. This is why line is more important than tone. It is capable of interpreting. A line has direction, dynamism, power — life.

This is probably the reason why humourous subjects often lose their effect when they are given the full tonal treatment. Somehow humour does not go hand in hand with an accurate and tight technique. I know there are probably hundreds of exceptions to this — Lawson Wood is one — but generally speaking humour seems to require simplicity and directness.

It has been a new experience for me recently to be involved in projects where humour and charm are more important than finish and precision. It has taught me about simplicity and restraint. It has taught me a lot about what to leave out, though I still revert now and then to an obsessive attention to irrelevant detail. I have an inborn compulsion to keep working away at things till they look finished or 'full'.

Anyway, I was only given six weeks in which to come up with about forty drawings for Mike Batt's project, so the time-factor effectively stayed my hand, and much of the work I did for this remained as sketches, uncorrupted by later careful additions.

I have subsequently developed some of this by tinting or re-painting, but it is still the rough sketches that please me most, particularly those in which I tried to develop engaging personalities for creatures that may (or may not) be Snarks.

For some of these drawings I first made models from white plasticine, the more easily to visualise the creatures from all angles. After much handling, the plasticine became distorted, broken and dirty, but by then I could manage fairly well without them. Finally I somehow retained the three-dimensional image in my visual memory and could mentally consult it any time I needed to.

Incidentally, when old, hardened plasticine needs to be softened for use, a good method is to leave it for a few minutes in tepid water. I have also found that old plasticine may to some extent be rejuvenated by being passed through an etching press!

Most of the ideas I produced for the Snark project were of course done

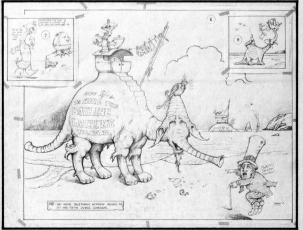

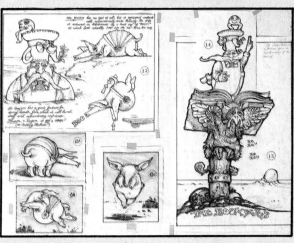

Above: *This is THE BOOJUM'S DIVING POOL, an idea emerging from the project 'The Hunting of the Snark' (1983), as did the sketches at the bottom of the two preceding pages.*

Black ink, applied with both pens and brushes, was the principle medium for the foreground in this sketch. The background, casually applied with an air-brush and deliberate spatter, was done while the foreground was protected by masking fluid. The paper was unfortunately of rather poor quality for this;

masking fluid should really only be used on smooth boards specially manufactured for fine work.

The Boojum himself — or is he a Snark? — was drawn on a separate piece of paper, cut out and stuck on later in the best position.

Below: *THE ACME BATHING MACHINE also came from the 'Snark' project. This cartoon, done mainly with Rapidograph and steel pens, betrays my profound admiration for William Heath Robinson — his technique with a pen as well as his sense of humour.*

THE "ACME" BATHING MACHINE

FOR THE USE OF PRE-BREAKFAST SWIMMERS
ON THOSE COLD WINTER MORNINGS

A SNARK IS...

...FUN-LOVING...

A MODEL PARENT...

...GOOD AT SPORT...

...INTELLIGENT...

...BALANCED...

...RELAXED...

...AN EXCELLENT SKATER...

...WELL - UPHOLSTERED...

...AN OBEDIENT AND AFFECTIONATE PET...

...BUT ~ UNLESS CORRECT BAIT IS USED...

...VERY HARD TO CATCH!!

Above:

When working on the 'Snark' project with Mike Batt in 1983 we never really decided what a Snark looked like. Indeed by tradition it is forbidden to represent him. I don't know what he looks like. I have never seen him. If I had, I should have already 'vanished away like midnight smoke'. This is only a 'potential Snark', one of many creatures — bandersnatches, boojums etc. — which appear fleetingly in Batt's adaptation of Carroll's poem.

Left:

Plasticine models can be useful in sketching — particularly when a character needs establishing 'in the round'.

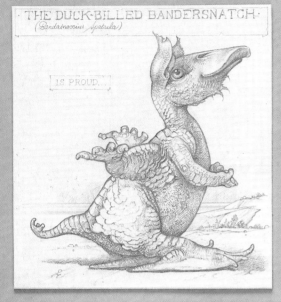

THE DUCK-BILLED BANDERSNATCH
(Bandasnaccius Spatrula)

IS PROUD...

FEARLESS...

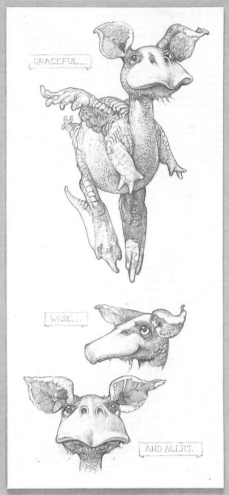

GRACEFUL...

WISE...

AND ALERT.

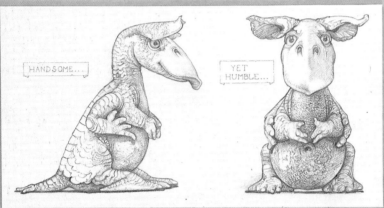

HANDSOME...

YET HUMBLE...

Above: *The Duck-billed Bandersnatch is one of many creatures in a large family, which includes Scottish as well as nocturnal variants. All of them have six limbs and an equable disposition.*

These sketches were done very quickly in pencil, using a Plasticine model as a reference (see preceding page).

Right: *Pencil drawings, when effectively mounted, make a good basis for watercolour and coloured-pencil work. A very hard pencil (5H) has been used here to add further detail, and small touches of white gouache provide occasional crisp highlights.*

(2A) "The Terrible Snidd" Patrick Woodroffe June 1985.

Above: *This visual pun (Snake + hark = Snark) is only a red herring! This is just another potential Snark, and must not be regarded as anything more than every musician's best friend — the good listener.*

The drawing as reproduced here originated in a tiny sketch, but had to be re-done on good quality board so that gouache, watercolour, inks and coloured pencils could be used to achieve sufficient contrast of colour and tone.

Below: *This helicopter pilot began as part of a pencil sketch, but was cut out and coloured up for possible inclusion as an embellishment in the 'Snark' album. Watercolours were used, as well as a very small amount of gouache. A hard pencil reinforced details after the tinting was dry.*

Above: *Many modifications were eventually made to this pencil sketch before it was finally transformed into the oil-painting destined for the cover of the album 'The Hunting of the Snark' (see page 85). The logotype was abandoned in favour of lettering 'chiselled from the sky'. The ship became much bigger, more 'romantic' in appearance. The girl was removed all together.*

Separate pencil sketches were made in preparation for this Boojum photo-call. Xerox copies of each figure were cut out and arranged in position. A further Xerox copy of this ensemble then provided a very adequate basis from which the eventual illustration — originally intended for the back of the album 'The Hunting of the Snark' — could be traced.

Unfortunately this idea was eventually abandoned, though the sketch of the Boojum's camera was coloured up for possible inclusion as an embellishment (see page 113).

without models of any sort, and this can often be the most liberated and effective way to work. To tie yourself down to some pre-formed concept of how a thing *should* look can easily prevent you from imagining how it *could* look. This is why these days I very rarely use reference material of any kind. At one time, particularly when working on urgent commissions, I used photographic references a lot, but I find that they tend to stultify the vision and to sterilize the imagination.

I firmly believe — particularly when illustrating any kind of fantasy — that it is a mistake to rely on anything other than your own visual memory. If photographs are ever used as references — and once again, never in fantasy — I prefer to use photographs I have taken myself. If an artist wants to show what only he has seen, then he must use only his own eyes.

I don't think strict accuracy is important, for if art is to offer us anything at all that is not to be found 'out there' or in photographs, then it can only come from those fortunate instances when the artist sees something not quite straight, when his visual memory fails him just a little. Getting it at least slightly *wrong* is, I believe, what art is all about. Getting it right on the other hand denies the artist's individuality and can only lead him into stultifying conformism — hard work for him and boring for everyone else.

Vigorous, spontaneous pen and ink work (Rapidograph and steel pen) destined for reproduction, can be effectively adjusted and corrected by adding small touches of thick white gouache. This can lead to very precise yet dynamic results, but it is unsuitable when permanence is a consideration, for the gouache will inevitably become less opaque in time.

This drawing THE FLYING LESSON (1985) was made into an 'Ex Libris' book-plate for my daughter Rosie.

The basic craft. Some useful tips on equipment, tinting, embossing etc..

Although it is the product of a mechanical printing process, an etching is nevertheless a uniquely hand-made item — a 'multiple original' printed by hand from a hand-made copper plate.

The technique is based on very simple principles, but takes years of experience to control. Even then, you are never absolutely sure of successful results. Here is a brief summary of the basic process:-

The drawing — in reverse and in negative tones — is done mainly with a needle on a copper plate coated with a special black 'ground'. It is then 'bitten' by being immersed in a mixture of hydrochloric acid and potassium chlorate, which cuts the lines into the copper to a depth and width dictated by the duration of the 'bite'. The plate is often successively re-grounded, re-needled and re-bitten to achieve the desired effect. At each of these 'states' a test print or 'proof' is taken.

The printing process begins by heating the plate and covering it with a stiff oil-based ink. After wiping, first with scrim and then with the bare hand, the ink remains lodged only in the etched lines, though a thin film of ink is left on the surface in places to achieve certain effects, and other areas may be darkened by teasing ink from the lines with a piece of muslin ('retroussage').

The paper must be softened overnight in water and each sheet dabbed dry with blotting paper before use. The press consists of two heavy rollers with a steel 'bed' carrying the inked plate between them; the paper is protected from the rollers by various thick felt 'blankets'. Gumstrip is used to tape the finished print to a board so that it will dry flat.

Only a very small number of prints are made — an 'edition' may be only twelve or even less — simply because of the limitations of the process. Copper is a comparatively soft metal, which means that the shallow lines — which give an etching its unique delicacy — are the first to be worn away by the rigours of the process. For this reason the lower numbers in an edition are usually considered superior and priced accordingly more highly.

It would be impossible to describe in one chapter the enormously varied and complex techniques of etching in all its many forms. At any event there

The plate was proofed only four times for this little etching, though it was bitten and re-worked many more times than that.

The first state establishes all the main lines. Subsequent applications of ground must be very thorough, otherwise existing lines may be missed and exposed to the acid once again, thus widening them too much.

Final tiny adjustments were made between the third and fourth states, involving bites of only a few seconds. This produces very delicate grey lines, which, although giving the etching its distinctive character, do wear away fairly rapidly in the printing process.

Some lines in the above proofs are in pencil — to help in re-working the plate. The fourth and final state is illustrated actual size.

This picture *A YULE VALENTINE (1980)* was printed onto a Truline board which was first lightly dampened with a sponge.

The snow-flakes were not spattered on but were placed individually with a brush.

Etchings may be effectively tinted with oils (as may ink drawings) provided the support is sound and a couple of coats of Liquin are applied as a base.

Preparing the plate:

Thick copper sheet (1) is cut with a sheet-metal saw (2), whereas thin soft copper (3) (as sold for roofing purposes) can easily be cut with tin-snips (4).

Dilute ammonia (5) and talc (6) are rubbed on the polished plate with two cloth pads to ensure that all grease is removed. After rinsing, it is preferable not to touch the plate again until the ground has been laid. For this reason I use a zinc spatula (7) to carry small plates to the hot-plate. Larger plates can be moved with a mole-wrench (8) provided the jaws are padded with pieces of card.

The Press:

My etching press was in several pieces and in a very bad way when given to me as scrap metal. While some heavy engineering work was being done on it, including several replacement parts, I was busy making the Japanese oak handles. It functioned extremely well, despite having no gearing at all. This can in fact be an advantage — if you're fairly strong — for geared presses do seem to take an unnecessarily long time.

The weight of such a press is colossal. The steel bed alone is a considerable burden for one man to carry. My press is at present installed in the attic, though I think the house would prefer it to be on the ground floor!

Much larger presses are of course available, but I have come to appreciate that other print-making techniques are perhaps better-suited to larger work.

Opposite page: In 1984 I spent part of that lovely hot summer producing a series of fourteen miniature etchings partially based on my own photographs of farm animals. The other seven appear on pages 42, 45 and 49.

This was a new departure for me, an attempt at 'going straight', and although I did manage to remain fairly faithful to Nature, I could not resist adding captions of my own.

The full collection was printed in an edition of only 24 and sold as a portfolio entitled TETHER TROUBLE.

The etchings are reproduced here approximately actual size.

· UNWELCOME · CURIOSITY ·

CHEWING THE CUD

AN · INSTANCE · OF · PRODIGAL · WASTE · IN · THE · DROUGHT · YEAR · 1984 ·

is already a vast amount of excellent literature on the subject, the best and most thorough being the Thames & Hudson guide by Walter Chamberlain.

Without books like his I myself could never have studied the processes, for I must confess that in fact I have never actually seen anyone else do these things. So although I am no kind of expert at all, I feel bound to take the trouble to follow Chamberlain's example, and to pass on a list of tips for those who have at least some knowledge of the subject, and to describe my experiences in areas which are perhaps my own, or which are to my knowledge not described in any of the well-known text-books.

The standard gauge polished copper sheet usually supplied for etching is essential for large prints, but I find that a thinner, unpolished copper (available locally from a yachting chandlers) is far cheaper and perfectly adequate for plates smaller than a hand's breadth. It can also be cut very easily with tin-snips rather than with a sheet-metal saw.

To ensure that the polished plate is kept thoroughly free of grease before the ground is laid, it is useful to manipulate it only with small wads of rag, using alternate hands to rub it with dilute ammonia and talc. I take special care to ensure that the edges are grease-free and I also clean the back of the plate. To thoroughly remove the ammonia and talc I dip the plate in clean water, and — especially when re-grounding an already-bitten plate — clean it with a stiff dish-brush kept only for this purpose. Grease or talc left on the plate can lead to a badly adhering or porous ground. To carry the clean plate to the hot-plate I use a piece of metal sheet or a mole-wrench with padded jaws.

My heater is in fact a crêpe-plaque with a very efficient thermostat. This is excellent for large plates, but for many years I did all my grounding and inking on an ordinary boiling ring. A good iron hot-plate is essential however for work over 200 millimetres in size, for uneven temperatures cause the plate to buckle.

I always lay the ground (hard dark) with a roller, but when re-grounding a plate that has already been bitten, it is essential to force the ground into all the etched lines with a leather dabber. To remove excess ground I run the roller over a separate sheet of warm metal. It is very important that the ground should be fairly thin — a pale, warm brown — and when re-grounding, I run the roller back and forth over the cooling plate in order to ensure that the sharp edges of the bitten lines are protected by ground. When hot, the ground seems to draw away from these sharp

FRUSTRATION

DROUGHT YEAR 1984

IMITATIVE PREENING

JUST BEFORE MILKING TIME

TETHER TROUBLE

HAMSTERS

THE SPOTTED SOW

Right:
Laying the ground:

My hotplate (1) is a large crêpe-plaque obtained locally from a supplier of hotel catering equipment. Thermostatically controlled and very stable, it is extremely appropriate for this job, though very expensive.

A small electric boiling ring (2) is perfectly adequate, provided the plate is only small. Care should be taken however that the ground does not become too hot and burn. Excess ground is removed from the plate with a roller and deposited on a warm metal plate nearby (3).

When re-grounding a plate, hard dark ground (4) must be forced carefully into all the bitten lines with a leather dabber (5).

Twisted tapers (6) are used to smoke the ground to darken and harden it. This is unnecessary when re-grounding a plate, for etched lines should be clearly visible through the ground. My home-made spring-loaded plate-holder (7) is invaluable when small plates need to be inverted for smoking.

Stop-out varnish (8) is removed with white spirit. Straw-hat varnish (9) dries more quickly and is removed with methylated spirit. Either of these may be used to protect the back of the plate or to mask sections out during biting. A brush permanently mounted in straw-hat varnish (10) saves a great deal of time cleaning brushes with meths.

Needling the plate:

A copper stylus (1) is preferable to a pencil for tracing directly through the sketch onto the grounded plate.

A soft dusting brush (2) is useful for periodically brushing away dust as the ground is needled.

I use two thicknesses of point (3) when needling. For comfort's sake, the handles are preferably padded — especially when stippling.

The plate is easily manipulated if mounted on a small piece of softboard (4). A pad covered with soft plastic sheet (5) protects the plate from the heat of the hand. This uniquely soft plastic (6) is also useful for backing any equipment that is likely to come into contact with the ground — templates for example (7) and T-square (8).

The spectacles have special prismatic lenses for very close work.

47

Below:
Pulling a proof:
Next to the hot-plate are stiff pads or 'forms' over which I stretch scrim or silk rags for wiping. In the foreground is my 'paper-clamp'. Lined with Formica, these boards can be weighted down so that stacks of damp paper can be stored between them. If left for any length of time, the paper is also wrapped in polythene.

Above:
Biting the Plate:

Acids can be very tricky. If a Dutch mordant mixture (hydrochloric acid and potassium chlorate) fails to work, it is a good idea to 'prime' it with waste copper scraps.

Acid baths can easily be made up cheaply by lining boxes with polythene sheet, though photographic dishes as shown here are far safer.

I never throw acid away, always adding the next mixture to what remains of the old. The acid gets consumed simply by evaporation and repeated rinsing of the plate.

My recipe for Dutch mordant is: 21oz. water, 6oz. hydrochloric acid and $1\frac{1}{4}$ oz. potassium chlorate.

Always add acid to water: never breathe in the vapour.

Left:

Gumstrip (1) is used to stick down the edges of the print on a piece of hardboard. A paperhanger's roller (2) is good for ensuring the adhesion is secure. The damp proof (3) is stuck down so that it will dry flat.

Small etched plates (4) can be mounted type-high and used for surface printing along with type etc. on a 'parlour press' (5). The captions for my etchings on pages 54 and 55, and also the label which I put on my portfolios of etchings were printed in this way. Line blocks (6) or logotypes can be made up inexpensively from photographically reduced artwork etched on zinc plates by a trade block-maker.

There's nothing like an agreeable itch.

119. 5th State.

The longer the tether the richer the milk.

A.10. Fourth State.

SS 11
2nd.
State.
30/8/84

OVER THE TOP!

Further proofs from my series of miniature etchings TETHER TROUBLE (1984).

Fairly thin copper sheet was used for these plates. It has many advantages for small plates: it is light, cheap and easy to cut into shape. If it is soft (annealed) copper, a little gentle hammering will harden it up.

Thin sheet is also preferable for small plates in that the plate-mark or bevel becomes obtrusive if the sheet is too thick.

edges, and if it is allowed to cool like this, the lines may be widened when the plate is re-bitten.

I only smoke the first application of ground. I leave all subsequent grounds unsmoked, which allows work already done — and the results of repeated later bites — to show up as dark lines. A specially prepared transparent ground is available for this, but I prefer to stick to the methods and materials I am used to.

It is useful, when grounding small plates, to manipulate them only with a broad metal spatula, which enables the roller to cover the whole surface with ground.

Inverting a large plate for smoking is always a problem, but for small plates I use a spring-loaded holder which I made specially for this purpose. This enables all areas of the plate to be smoked without spoiling the ground.

I always use thin paper for preparatory sketches; this means that I can transfer the image to the plate simply by pencilling the back of the sketch and tracing it. For tracing I use a home-made copper stylus for greater accuracy and in order not to spoil the sketch with further pencil marks. To locate the sketch accurately over the plate I cut V-slots, and stick it down with small pieces of Sellotape placed over the holes; this does not damage the sketch and the slots are easily re-closed.

To protect the ground from the heat of my hand and from friction while I work, I use a pad faced with a very soft plastic foam which seems to be otherwise only used to wrap hi-fi equipment. I have also faced my home-made etching square and templates with this unique material.

For very close work I use specially prescibed prism spectacles, which are designed not only to give a slight magnification, but also to combat the fatigue and head-aches brought on by constant converging of the eyes.

Eye-strain apart, it is preferable to work fairly small for several reasons: all the processes and equipment are not only more manageable but also very much cheaper. Small hot-plate — less electricity. Small acid-bath — less acid. Small press — cheaper blankets. Small plates — less wasted paper, smaller, more easily-corrected mistakes. Not only that, I firmly believe that most really good etchings are very small anyway. There is something inherent in the process that seems to favour smallness.

I always use Dutch mordant to bite the plate, though I have had some disasters when having to re-stock with hydrochloric acid. If a new mixture won't bite properly, or if it eats away the ground instead of the lines, it should be 'primed' by having some copper waste dissolved in it. I always make thorough tests on grounded

This plate THE RUNAWAY BULL (1985) measures 228×393mm. and is the companion or pendant of THE PROUD FATHER shown overleaf. The sketches for these etchings were finished in pen and ink (see page 27). The two plates were worked on in tandem, so that while I was perhaps waiting for some stop-out varnish on one to dry or for its ground to cool, I could work on the other and not be held up.

Before printing the edition (50 prints), I experimented with various combinations of inks. The edition itself was printed in black, with a very small addition of burnt sienna.

The plate has in some places been wiped very clean with the finger (in the crook of the tree where the bird sits and on the bull's forehead, for example) but elsewhere (in deep shade and in the foliage) the ink has been teased out of the lines with a muslin rag to give a richer black (retroussage).

The motto reads:
'The smoke from the fire just flies away
The tide leaks through to the narrow bay;
If you read the assassin's false pretence
Get you gone to a field that has no fence.'

copper scraps before using a new batch of mordant. The alternative is a recipe for disappointment and disaster.

Computer print-out paper is excellent for proofing. Only for editions do I use expensive cartridge or hand-made paper. Satisfactory prints can also be made on white, coloured or even metallic mounting board.

When printing an edition, a stack of soaked paper may be partially dried by working a roller over the top sheet. This means less blotting paper is needed to prepare the paper for printing.

During printing, the damp paper needed for the edition can be wrapped in polythene and/or kept in a 'paper-clamp'. Mine is made from plywood faced with Formica.

To mark the position of the plate(s) on the press bed I use a paper diagram taped to the bed and covered with a polythene sheet. The polythene cleans easily with white spirit between each pull, but will eventually stretch and need replacing. I always have a stock of polythene sheets cut ready and to hand; they need replacing after about ten prints.

When printing editions, I always do as many plates as possible at once, which means that dirty parts of the process, like inking and hand-wiping, can be kept separate from clean ones, like stretching prints and handling paper. I clean my hands with Swarfega as I go from one process to another. I printed the whole edition of all fourteen plates of 'Tether Trouble' in this way.

Dressed (hard) scrim is very effective for preliminary wiping when wrapped over a padded former.

Frustrating scratches on the plate are often caused either by filings left over after sawing and bevelling or by hard fragments in the scrim. Scrim pads may be softened by rubbing them on the sharp edge of a table; tapping will cause hard abrasive particles to fall out.

Silk or nylon rags stretched over a former are excellent for clean final wiping if this is required. These cloths can be cleaned in white spirit and re-used after washing in detergent.

When hand-wiping, an old towel worn round the waist is a good way to remove excess ink from the hands from time to time.

When taping prints down with gum-strip it is useful to press the edges with a paper-hanger's roller. This helps to prevent the print coming adrift and distorting as it dries.

Copper plates may be cut and mounted type-high for use with ordinary metal type, but it must be remembered that when etched lines are to appear as white on black, they need to be much wider and deeper if they are not going to fill with ink and disappear.

Prints from etched plates are

THE PROUD FATHER (1985) is the companion piece to THE RUNAWAY BULL shown on the preceding pages.

The motto reads:

'If only the year would stay its clock
In the term when the farmer spares his stock,
When even the mightiest cleaves to the meak
And even a dumb beast's tongue may speak.'

It was proofed eight times before I was satisfied with it. Each proofing probably represents four or five bites, between each of which the plate was re-worked, the newly etched lines being visible through the ground. Last to be drawn were the shadows of leaves on the bull's rump. This was a tricky operation, for mistakes are hard to eradicate from an etched plate. They must be laboriously scraped and polished away, and even a shallow line can take a long time.

The sketch appears on page 27.

· IF ONLY THE YEAR WOULD STAY ITS CLOCK · IN THE YEAR WHEN THE FARMER SPARES HIS STOCK · WHEN EVEN THE MIGHTIEST CLEAVES TO THE MEEK · AND EVEN A DUMB BEAST'S TONGUE MAY SPEAK ·

This triplet of etchings was a product of that strange drought summer of 1984, when the sun-gilded countryside seemed to take on a strange alien mystery. Somehow anything seemed possible. Pan, the great god Pan, hid behind every hedgerow.

The verses (with etched, type-high cartouches) were printed on my small Adana hand press, and the whole edition of 50 prints mounted in gold-embossed card. The gold mounting boards were polished with a mixture of wax varnish and burnt sienna etching ink.

Let's go to the meadow where Pan has stood:
And we'll stop by the edge of the wood,
And we'll mark with a wiggledy apple-tree root
The spot where he planted his cloven boot—
But be quick, ere the sun dries the mud!

A yellow fur doth dandify thy face,
thou very cockscomb of a flower!
When children puff thy balding mace,
thy flying hairs shall tell the hour.

54

Another pair of etchings from 1984. Once again the plates were worked on simultaneously so as to avoid delays.

The verses, as well as those on the opposite page, are taken from the first draft of a 'romance in the antique manner' which I wrote during that beautiful summer.

cheaper than bromides, and may be used very satisfactorily as black copy embellishments for paste-ups, especially when a large 'library' of imagery is needed. Bromides do however offer the capability of reducing the artwork in order to tighten up the drawing.

A plate may be specially designed so that prints from it may be cut and fitted together to form multiple images of great complexity, though in projects of this sort very accurate planning is essential, and all prints must stretch and dry to the same degree if they are to fit together properly.. It is well worth the effort however, for it is extraordinary how repetition can sometimes increase the power of an image.

Etchings may be tinted with watercolours or drawing ink. A very weak coat of size helps to overcome the difficulty of getting the watercolour to take, especially where the lines are very close together. Inks do not present this problem, in fact they go on extremely easily, but if permanence is important they should be avoided, for they tend to fade rather quickly.

Etchings may be tinted far more effectively with oils. For a good firm support, prints may be made (with only a very thin blanket) on 'Truline' board or similar. When the ink is thoroughly dry — after several weeks — the print should be given two or more coats of 'Liquin' medium. When dry, this provides an excellent surface for very bright glazes in the same medium. The relief of the intaglio print remains perfectly intact on a fine illustration board, and when tinted gives the effect almost of cloisonnée enamel. Permanence — so far — seems to be no problem with this technique.

'Open bite' — when large areas of copper are allowed to be corroded — is a useful technique for producing embossed work which can be incorporated into paintings to provide startling realism.

Etched plates may also be used to emboss boards coated with kitchen foil (which gives a fair imitation of cast metal), to produce 'antique finish' mounts for prints, or simply as a method of rendering metallic titling etc.. When mounting foil for embossing it is advisable to use the minimum amount of adhesive and to allow it plenty of time to dry. It is surprising what damage even tiny amounts of glue can do under the pressure of the press.

Embossing metallic mounting board is only successful on a small scale. Huge pressures are needed to obtain a deep enough penetration on fine work, and this will only show up when polished for example with a mixture of etching ink and wax varnish which lodges around the marks.

Metallic titling etc. can be

produced by concealing the unetched surface of the plate by repeated applications of ink or oil-paint from a roller. Strangely enough this technique yields results far less impressive than the work of a good titling specialist who understands how to paint metal.

Above:

Provided fairly thin strong paper is used, etching is an excellent way of providing multiple black and white copy for use as embellishments on paste-ups for books.

Most of my books have been decorated in this way, but these days I tend to opt for a less cluttered design. They are stuck down with the usual 'Cow' gum.

Left:

A carefully designed plate may produce a circular repeating image, as shown here in this illustration for 'The Pentateuch' (1979). Entitled THE VICIOUS CIRCLE, it is intended to show the absurd self-destructive futility of war.

The cut or join may in fact be quite simple, disguised by lines that cross over it. The shape of the plate itself is unimportant. The assemblage of prints is actually 515mm. in diameter, but as shown above in the violet border, it was reproduced much smaller in the book.

For 'The Pentateuch' (1979) I made two illustrations to represent trumps of light and darkness. The sketches were made with a carefully designed, almost diagonal border-line, and traced onto the plates first one way, then upside down, keeping the centre-point in position.

V-slots cut in the sketches enable small pieces of Sellotape to be used to stick them down.

Each way up the trumps have a subtly different reading, for both the ideograms and the illustrations are changed. The trump of beacons, shown here approximately actual size, symbolizes the transition from day to night — an important time for a civilisation existing on floating marine cities.

The malevolent Ildrinn (below) is depicted as the thief of light. Her beacon projects only darkness. Her mantle snuffs out the last lamp.

Heavy cartridge paper was used for these proofs, for the tinting was done almost entirely in watercolour. The bright cerise however, is an ink.

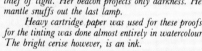

The etching NO PLACE FOR THE NAIVE (1981) was produced specifically for the lyric it illustrates in 'Hallelujah Anyway'. It was first printed on Truline board, then tinted with oils. On the left it is shown as it later appeared when I produced a tinted (watercolour) edition of the re-worked plate. The elaborate card mount was produced as surface prints from etched plates.

Liquin, on oleo-resin medium produced by Winsor & Newton, provides the perfect means of tinting etchings with oils. The etching must however be printed on a good quality smooth board.

Phenomenal control of the colour is possible, not only in thin glazes, but also when applying tiny drops of colour from a pointed brush.

The scrollwork on this illustration for 'Hallelujah Anyway' reads: 'Love is the treasure-house of happiness — guard it well!'

AMOR · EST · OPES · FELICITATIS · CUSTODITE

Patrick Woodroffe del et sculp. June 1980. (334 E)

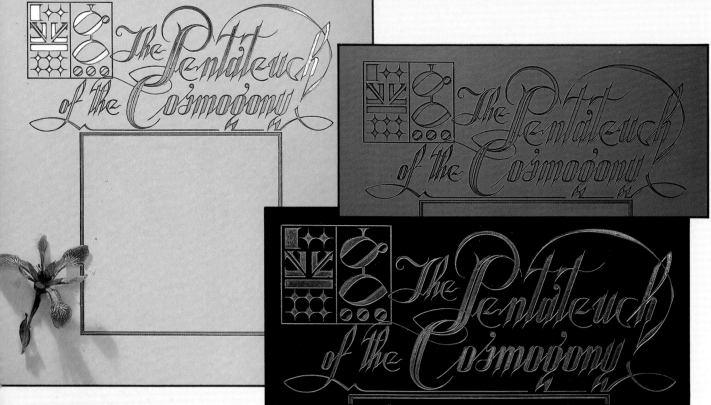

Above:

My original design for the cover of 'The Pentateuch' consisted partly of a photograph of the above etched copper plate. On the left the polished plate is shown after white oil-paint had been applied to the surface with a roller.

Top right is the polished metal plate, and below that the same plate after black ink had been applied to the surface.

The alien bloom was made up from three types of genuine garden flower. It also appears in the painting FOREST KINGDOM (see page 72).

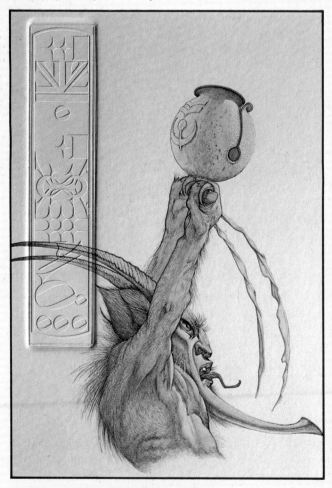

This illustration of the storm-god Beltempest ('The Pentateuch' 1979) shows how Truline board may be embossed. Only slight dampening is needed on the surface. For this purpose card is more effective than blankets between board and top roller. It minimises distortion of the back of the board from pressure.

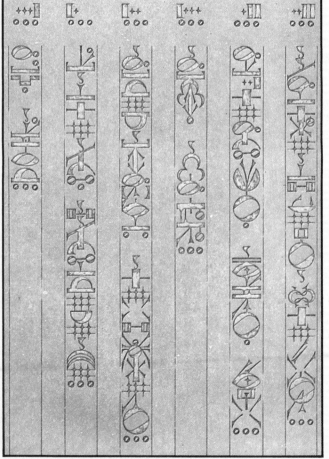

This cryptic alien text for 'The Pentateuch' was produced from an etched plate inked red in the intaglio and given a surface application of blue from a roller.

Right:

In this detail from MOONDANCE ('The Pentateuch' 1979), a thick impasto of white oil-paint imitates the relief of the embossed board.

The symbols represent the Sun God, beginning and end. (Detail slightly enlarged.)

Below:

Aluminium foil may also be effectively embossed when mounted first on fairly thick card. These are the headings for the five books of 'The Pentateuch'.

Right:

For Christmas 1983 I produced an edition of 60 of this rather lavish card, thirty of which were tinted in watercolours. Gold-faced board was embossed for the mounts, which were polished with a mixture of wax varnish and etching ink.

Christus natus est!

Proof extra to Edition. P.W.

*Acrylic, watercolour, coloured pencils,
inks, marbling, air-brush etc..
Fast techniques for fast results, where
permanence is of secondary importance.*

Publication deadlines largely dictate what techniques are available to the illustrator, and although there is no doubt in my mind that oils — alone or in combination with other media — offer the greatest possibilities for contrast and richness of colour and tone, it is very often impossible to use them for illustration purposes simply because of the slowness of the process.

For several years during the rock and SF boom of the early seventies, I earned my living almost entirely from illustrating book-jackets, and because the time available for each commission would often be as little as three days — I once did two covers in one week — it was essential to learn a quick, mainly water-based technique which could still give high contrast and strong colour.

Using masking fluid, air-brush, marbling and so on, it is possible to treat the background and foreground of a picture as totally separate tasks, thus enabling very smooth or very textured areas to emphasize more important areas of tighter detail.

For this type of work I have generally used Daler 'Truline' board, a high-quality cardboard faced with a very smooth paper on one side. This is not only a very sympathetically 'giving' surface on which to do all the preliminary drawing, but it also has enough strength to stand up to the rough treatment it may get — particularly during marbling. Before using it I bind all the cut edges with gumstrip so that the corners do not lift; this also gives extra strength.

I have a very simple method of transfering the preliminary pencil sketch to the board, but it will only work if the paper is thin enough. I do all my sketches on the type of paper used for computer print-outs, which is not only thin and strong, but also stands up quite well to rubbing, folding, wetting etc.. This paper also has the advantage of lightness, which makes it very good when roughs have to be sent through the post.

The sketch — protected on the face by a coat of fixative — is turned over and the back thoroughly blackened with a grade B or HB pencil. A thick graphite stick is probably quicker, but I usually save my pencil stubs for this purpose rather than throw them away. I tape the sketch lightly in position on the board and trace over all necessary parts of the drawing so that the graphite is

Below:
Between 1973 and 1976 I produced approximately 90 book-cover paintings. A rough, like this one for 'The Seedbearers' (1975), was usually submitted to the art-director well in advance, but tight schedules usually meant that finished artwork had to be produced at break-neck speed. Each of the pictures on this spread took only three days.

Deep contrasts were achieved here by working in watercolour, ink and coloured pencils on top of a roughly painted undercoat of waterproof gouache. Titanium white gouache highlights were added later, and black Indian ink was finally used to deepen contrasts.

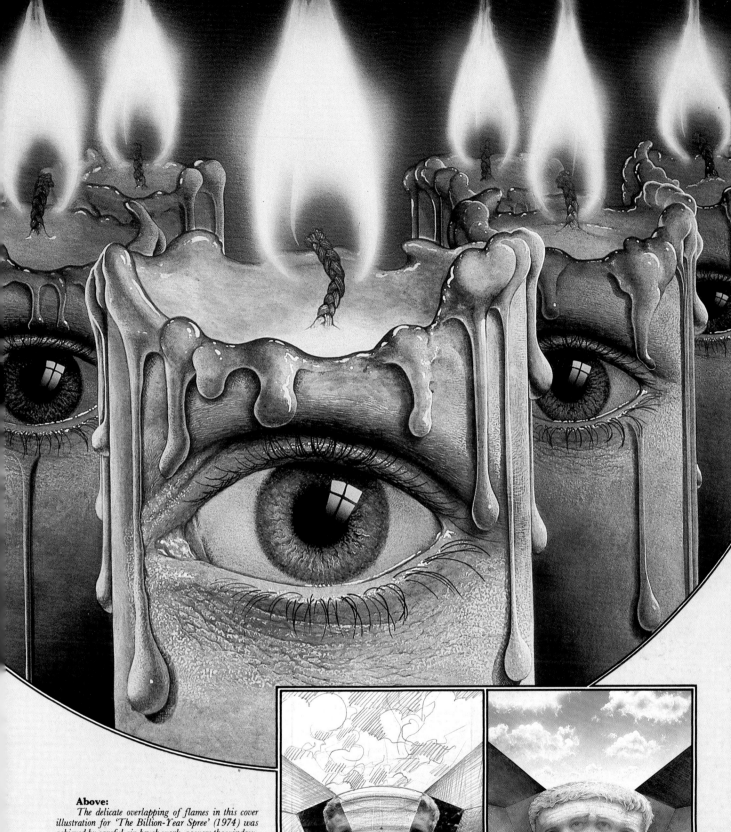

Above:
  The delicate overlapping of flames in this cover illustration for 'The Billion-Year Spree' (1974) was achieved by careful air-brush work, as were the window-reflections in the eyes, but most subtleties of colour — the browning of the iris around the pupil, the hint of pale blue at the base of the flame — were the result of gentle coloured-pencil work.
  (Detail approximately actual size.)

Above:
  The need to turn out ideas and finished artwork very quickly means that you sometimes produce images you don't feel very very proud of. This curious idea for 'The New Adam' (1973) does however illustrate the relationship between the first idea and the way it is ultimately realized.

The foreground was applied in thick (almost dry) gouache to get a good texture; shadows were then added with the air-brush, the sunlit part protected by a simple paper mask.

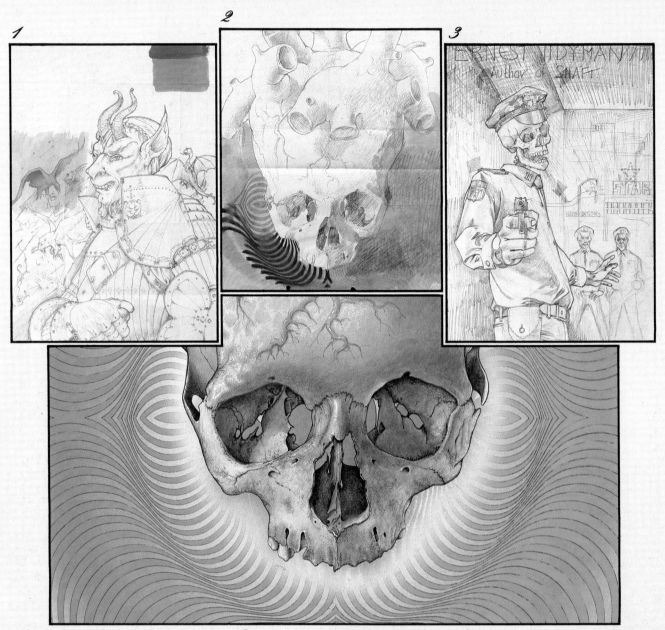

1 For 'The Guns of Avalon' (1975) waterproof acrylic gouache proved particularly useful. Not only does it spray well in an air-brush — I tested the sky colours on the sketch — but the blues, greens and reds which I used in the eyes, are intense and opaque enough to be used almost like oils. All dark areas (the neck, the shadows in the armour) were reinforced with waterproof black ink applied in tiny hatched lines.

2 The 'op art' background of 'The Stagnation of the Heart' (1973) was drawn with a card template rotating on a central point. Alternate lines were painted in with emerald green gouache, then, after some final spray-work, the skull itself was painted last.

3 For 'Line of Duty' (1975) the art-director at Transworld Books insisted that I alter the position of the head.

This illustration was eventually copied in every detail — even my mistakes — and used illegally on the cover of a magazine in Brazil.

The rock-band Judas Priest had planned to call their album 'Sad Wings of Destiny', but eventually chose the title 'Fallen Angels' (1975).

The background here was first marbled then modified with acrylic gouache to suggest the flames and smoke of Hell.

It is a good idea to send only Xerox copies of roughs to the art directors. This means that you already have the sketch ready for tracing when your roughs have been approved.

offset from the back of the sketch onto the board. This is usually done with a sharp, hard (say 4H) pencil, but I prefer a home-made copper stylus, which needs sharpening far less often and will give much more accurate results. Copper also has the advantage of leaving only a feintly visible trace on the sketch, which means that you can just see what parts you have done, and not have to go over it again. This surely must be one of the most numbingly boring tasks an artist has to fulfil, but if it is carefully and accurately done, it saves a great deal of work.

Once the tracing is finished I carefully re-draw and improve the sketch until I am satisfied that nothing is amiss. Even though every bit of this work will eventually be obscured, I think it is essential that this drawing should be as accurate as possible, for drastic over-painting is not easy with water-based techniques, nor is it usually possible to scrape away serious errors.

The completed pencil drawing is then sprayed with fixative, which must be allowed to dry off thoroughly before the next stage.

A generous coat of masking fluid (liquid frisket) is then applied to any areas I want to keep thoroughly clean for later detailed work. This usually — but not necessarily — means the foreground. Masking fluid is put on with a soft watercolour brush, although a steel dip-pen can be used for fine lines. Brushes used for this should be old ones kept specially for the purpose, because no matter how clean they are kept, they always suffer when a build-up of congealed fluid has to be periodically removed.

It is unnecessary to use masking fluid to cover all the areas that need to be protected; large areas can be covered with sheets of paper taped to the dry fluid. If there is only a little simple air-brush work to be done, these pieces of paper can be simply held in place with weights. I keep a selection of lead-sheet snippings for this purpose.

A simple graded tone makes a highly effective background for elaborate foreground work, but I have very often combined air-brush with other techniques in order to achieve a more dynamic background.

Rough brushwork for example can be very effective when softened, neatened up or almost obscured by smoothly graded air-painting. On the other hand the roughness seems to take away that mechanical feeling that can sometimes de-humanise work done with air-brush alone.

Acrylic gouache is particularly suitable for this, because it dries very quickly and it is easy to build up a good texture in a short time. I use a square-ended flat sable brush, sometimes with the paint fairly wet, sometimes almost dry, depending on what effect I want.

Once dry, acrylic gouache can be roughly brushed over and generally messed about without fear of it lifting or rubbing away. It dries with a good matt texture and makes an excellent surface to which further detail may be applied later.

Common household emulsion is also very good for backgrounds, especially when only a simple black or grey is needed. Black emulsion makes a good base on which to spray further air-brush atmospherics to illustrate a night sky for example.

Stars may be spatered on from a tooth-brush loaded with a fairly stiff mixture of white. Good quality titanium white gouache is preferable to household emulsion for detailed work, because it is both more opaque and more finely ground. Spattering is best done from above, though care must be taken that large drips do not fall off the brush and ruin the work. It is also advisable to protect a wide area of adjacent floor with newspaper. The tooth-brush is held with the bristles uppermost and the thumb is drawn back over them so that they spring up in succession.

While spraying, brushing or spattering the background, it is possible to use masks cut from acetate or paper. 'Kodatrace' is an acetate sheet frosted on one side so that it may be drawn on before cutting. This is wonderful for very detailed masks, because it does not buckle or expand when wet, but quite often a paper mask may do a simple job very well.

Marbling provides extremely dynamic and amorphous backgrounds for illustrations, especially when used in combination with air-brush and other techniques. It is also extremely useful for producing interesting titling, mounts, decorative boxes and portfolios.

There are several methods, though I have found none more satisfactory for my needs than the quickest and cheapest. The genuine old-fashioned techniques using sea-weed size, alum, ox-gall etc. need study and practice; the physics and chemistry are complex and demand great control over the conditions and materials.

My colours are generally only ordinary enamel paints floated on clean tap-water. My marbling trough is just a collapsible wooden frame supporting a heavy-duty polythene sheet on a white table-top. It happens to be a tilting table-top, so I can empty out the water without using a syphon. The white surface enables the marbled pattern to be visible as it forms.

I use the paints well-stirred but usually undiluted, splashing small droplets here and there all over the water. I then blow and puff where I want the floating droplets to expand or recede; I stir it around, puff and blow some more perhaps, then, when

In DEPARTURE FOR DARKNESS (from 'The Pentateuch' 1979), careful planning was essential. The space-ships had to be precisely the correct shape, and accurate acetate masks had to be made for the air-brush work.

The background was painted first with one flat coat of Dulux emulsion. Meanwhile of course, the foreground was protected by masking fluid. A disc of Kodatrace (acetate sheet) was placed over the moon area while the stars were spattered on from a tooth-brush.

Once the lower part of the sky had been air-brushed with blue and violet gouache, most of the remaining work was finished with a conventional sable brush. Subtle additions of high colour — like the brown lip of the launch crater — were made in watercolour.

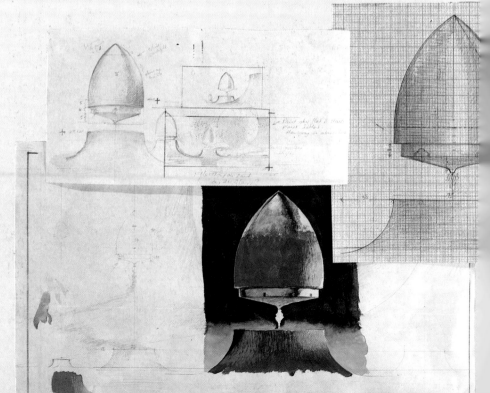

everything looks good, place the board face down in the trough, bowing it slightly in the middle, so that the whole board comes into contact with the surface.

It may need a second dip to give a more concentrated or complex pattern, especially if large areas of white remain exposed, but as soon as the marbling is done, the water must be shaken off quickly before it can damage the surface or the edges of the board. It is then thoroughly dried, preferably very quickly in front of a fire.

The air-brush can now be used to modify the result as much as required, but this too should be done quickly, so that all masking fluid etc. can be peeled off carefully before the enamel paint has hardened so much that it won't come off.

The enamels should not be diluted with white spirit because this may attack the masking fluid and turn it into a messy solution that will ruin the drawing underneath. The dried masking fluid should stretch and peel away easily like a thin rubber sheet, but some areas may need special attention from a rubber or even a scalpel.

Marbling — particularly over a drawing — is one of the many techniques that can only be learned by experience. There is always a potential for disaster, but it is surprising how much can be improved upon or concealed by later work.

If no marbling is done, then the masking fluid can be left on for as long a time as is needed to work on the background. This means that detailed additions made after the first coat of paint may in turn be sprayed over to give atmospheric perspective. Underlying simple brushwork — one stroke of a two-inch household paint-brush to render the sea or a beach for example — may be overlaid with successive additions of detail.

The effect of rain may be achieved by dragging parallel lines across the sky with a very dry brush of watery colour. Clouds and atmospherics may be 'scumbled' in with an almost dry brush. The sun's rays may be built up layer by layer with radial masks, and in all these cases — providing only acrylic gouache is used — the underlying paint will not dissolve or mix with later layers.

Rowneys unfortunately no longer supply the acrylic gouache which I used in all these pictures, I believe because it tends to solidify in the tubes, but a good substitute is to mix their excellent designer's gouache colours with a small amount of their acrylising medium. This is an essential precaution, for if the colours used are waterproof, it is possible to use layer after layer of thin paint, one on top of the other, to rub, spatter or sponge it successively without disturbing what is

Below:

As illustrated in this close-up from 'Universe Five' (1975), waterproof acrylic gouache is an excellent medium not only for broad air-brushed skies, but also for fine details like the thinly-pencilled whiskers of titanium white applied here with a No. 00 sable brush.

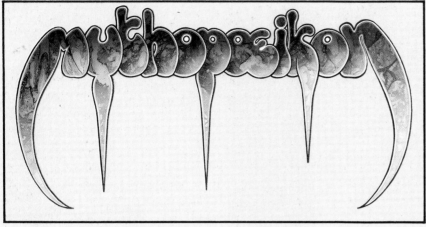

Opposite page, top:
In this detail from 'Three Hearts and Three Lions' (1974), the background was marbled in the traditional manner — with specially prepared colours and a size mixture made with Irish moss seaweed. As I found to my cost, this is a difficult technique to learn without personal help. I now rely on easier, though perhaps less spectacular methods.

Opposite page, lower left:
For 'Red Harvest' (1973) the sky area was marbled with a white polyurethane house-paint. This tends to spread in curious little clots and curds very reminiscent of galactic clouds.

Opposite page, lower right:
In 'Dwellers in the Mirage' (1973) a dynamic background was made in spite of things going wrong in the marbling. Twice-dipped, at one stage the paint hung off in folds!
In the foreground, thick 'dry-brushed' gouache makes a good base for later details.

Above:
This unpublished titling for my book 'Mythopoeikon' (1976) was first drawn in pencil on Truline board and the background painted out with protective masking fluid. The whole was then marbled and later modified with air-brush etc.
(Approximately 60% actual size.)

Below:
Marbling is an extremely quick and easy method for embellishing papers and boards for a multitude of uses. It is excellent not only for boxes and portfolios, but also for decorative mounts and slips for etchings.

already there.

The main virtue of acrylic gouache is the strength of colour and opacity which it offers, but where it really works well is when a glazing of transparent watercolour has been added later, where coloured pencils have been used on top of it to make subtle gradations, or where coloured or black inks have been used to add depth and contrast. This is where the mixed media technique as I have developed it most closely approaches oil-painting. Very thin layers of colour, some transparent, some opaque, are used to modify each other by fine adjustments of contrast and texture.

Watercolour lends itself very well to finely-detailed work, for the colour may be put on in tiny strokes with a very fine brush, slowly building in strength until satisfactory. As a glaze or to render fine detail it also has another advantage — it may be gently washed out or adjusted with a damp brush, and irreparable mistakes are rare. Strong opaque highlights — like the bright sparkle in an eye or a drop of blood — may be added on top of this with titanium white gouache.

Further air-brush work may be needed as a final touch — reflections in glass or subtle additions to atmospherics and tone — but usually the fine watercolour brushwork is the last thing to be done.

Coloured pencils — unless of the water-soluble type — should not be used where it is planned to add further detail in watercolour, for they have a wax constituent that renders this almost impossible.

As in most techniques, it is safest to use all water-based paints as thinly as possible and not to build up too many layers of different types of paint. Heavily built-up layers of any paint are liable to break down and flake off, and the more disparate the media used, the more likely it is that incompatibilities will arise and cause eventual changes.

However it must be said that the safest methods do not always produce the most striking immediate effects, and when the work in hand is an urgent commission in which permanence is not a requirement of the client, you can't always afford to be as careful as you should.

Watercolour and gouache paintings should always be protected from strong daylight, for even when the colours used are fairly permanent, they tend to be used so thinly that they can fade quite quickly.

Watercolour applied on top of acrylic gouache seems far less liable to attract fungal growth than when it is applied to paper or board directly. I assume this is because it is to some extent isolated from the organic and rather hygroscopic constitutents of the paper.

Below:
In THE DEATH OF GLASS ('The Penta-teuch' 1979), a large flat sable was used to put in the sky and sea. The sunbeams were air-brushed over a series of radial masks.
The vapour-trial in the sky was built up gradually with acrylic gouache applied with successively finer sables. (Slightly reduced.)

Below:
In this close-up of part of WALKING ALONG A ROAD THROUGH THE SKY ('Tinker' 1977) transparent watercolours were used over acrylic gouache for the grass and masonry.
The clouds were achieved with a very small amount of dilute gouache applied in repeated dabbings. Because the gouache is waterproof, it will build up readily into feathery and delicate forms. (Approximately actual size.)

Left:

This distant landscape is a detail of the background of *THE ORIENTAL DRAGON-FLY (1977)*. To depict the curtains of falling rain, very dilute gouache was repeatedly dragged over the sky, using a T-square to ensure that all the strokes were parallel. (Slightly enlarged).

Below:

Detail from *THE MINSTREL ('The Pentateuch'* 1979).

This alien sky demonstrates quite well how soft feathery clouds may be built up by repeated touches of white acrylic gouache applied very dilute yet with an almost dry brush.

Above:

This was my second attempt to arrive at a cover that would satisfy Pan Books (for Dashiell Hammett's 'Red Harvest' 1973) as well as myself. In the end neither was used anyway.

The symbolic representation of gang warfare as a closed circle preaches a somewhat similar sermon to that of THE VICIOUS CIRCLE (see pages 56 and 57). I don't think paperback covers are supposed to preach. Perhaps that is why it was never used.

The background texture results from fairly rough brushwork, softened subsequently by air-brush highlights and shadows.

Below:

In this close-up of HELP! HELP! ('Tinker' 1979) very fine sable brushes (000) were used to achieve tiny details. Highlights put in with acrylic gouache were tinted and adjusted with further touches of watercolour. The jacket was done by glazing brown watercolour over a fairly light gouache undercoat.
(Approximately actual size.)

Above:

Phenomenal contrast of colour is possible with good quality gouache paints, though very tight detail can only be achieved when watercolours are used on top as a glaze.

The exotic flowers in the foreground appeared not only in this detail from FOREST KINGDOM ('The Pentateuch' 1979), but also in my first design for the album cover (see page 60).
(Detail approximately actual size.)

Opposite page:

This detail from WAR ('The Pentateuch' 1979) demonstrates very well how fine details can be put in by glazing waterproof acrylic with watercolour.
(Approximately actual size.)

Right:
Waterproof designer's gouache is no longer available, but a good equivalent can be made by adding acrylic medium to ordinary gouache colour. These colours are extremely bright and opaque — excellent for covering other colours.

Small reversible dippers made from sea-shells or ceramic make very useful reservoirs for waterproof colours. The conical section allows only minimal evaporation.

Left:
The air-brush does not always function smoothly. Spatter can however be used creatively to blow inks or watercolour over the background to make dynamic spidery patterns.

Right:
Spatter can also be achieved with a tooth-brush. This is a good method for stars etc., but can also be used repeatedly to build up interesting textures.

Always mask clean areas carefully as well as the surrounding floor. It is surprising how far it can go.

Left:
Building up gouache with an almost dry brush. Waterproof acrylic gouache is perfect for feathery scumbles, where layer after layer is built up for clouds etc. It will not pick up or rub out in successive coats.

Right:
Reinforcing blacks with Indian ink.
A disadvantage of all water-based media is that they cannot get the degree of contrast that oils can. The dark areas can however be enriched by gradually building up thin dilute layers of Indian ink applied with a fine brush.

Opposite page, top:

This complex fur pattern would be impossible without very fine brushes. The black touches were added last of all in Indian ink.
(Detail from FOREST KINGDOM 1979, approximately actual size.)

Opposite page, bottom:

Delectably transparent and juicy blood drips from this heraldic eye in 'The Sailor on the Seas of Fate' (1976). The highlights are each made up from a small touch of blue (the reflection of the sky) followed by an even smaller touch of white (the reflection of the sun).

Below:

Small puffs of white from the air-brush were added to give a little glow to these spattered stars in *FALSE ARRIVALS* ('The Pentateuch' 1979).

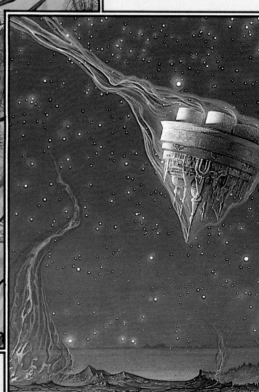

Above:

Brown ink was blown about across the background in this detail from *MISCHIEF* ('The Pentateuch' 1979). This was done several times — with some air-brushing in between for atmospheric perspective — to make a suitably chaotic setting for Ildrinn and her winged spider.
(Detail slightly reduced.)

1  *2*  *3*

The series THE TIGER AND THE DOVE was produced to illustrate the transition from war to peace in 'The Pentateuch' (1979).

Attempting animation with still images, I started at both ends of this series to produce the six illustrations *above. They demonstrate very well how opaque gouaches may be applied on top of each other — even repeatedly — without disturbing underlying work. The two pictures that remained when the process was finished were of course numbers 4 and 5.*

Detail from A WORTHY DESTINY (1979). The marbling on the columns in the background were faked with a fine sable brush and spattered from a tooth-brush. Subsequent air-brushing gave roundness to the columns and further tone to the background.

All the brighter colours are acrylic, though rarely used without watercolour additions. God's flesh was rendered in acrylic, followed by both watercolour and coloured pencil.

4

Final condition of the first picture.

5

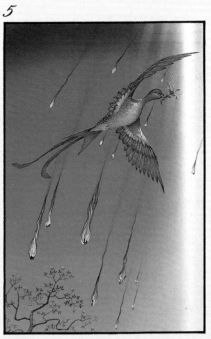

Final condition of the second picture.

6

This image was altered retrogressively to produce the preceding one.

Below:
   Acrylic gouache lends itself very well to fast work. It is coarse enough to receive subsequent work in coloured pencil; in this way very subtle extra colouring can be added easily and 'dry'.
   This gruesome subject-matter (a detail from 'Neq the Sword' 1974) is only a very small part of a three-in-one cover painting I had to complete in only ten days.

Above:
   Detail from 'Seven Footprints to Satan' (1975).
   Once again marbling was used here to provide a dynamic background and give extra vigour and fluidity to my painted flames.

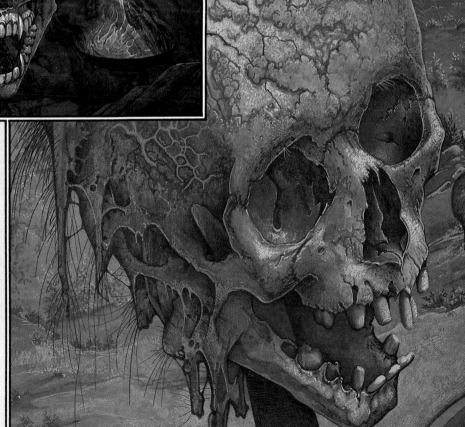

Below:
Detail from THE ORIENTAL DRAGON-FLY (1977). For soft highlights acrylic gouache can be put on very dilute. Because it dries immediately, further dilute touches enable graded tones to be built up slowly. Tiny specks of stiff white are then added to give a crisp sparkle.

Above:
This detail from A WORTHY DESTINY (1979) shows very little use of the air-brush. It was used only for the tonal change on the edge of the step, the arches reflected in the fish-bowl and to give roundness to the columns.

Above:
A sponge loaded with gouache was used to get the effect of erupting mud in this detail from FALSE ARRIVALS ('The Pentateuch' 1979). Highlights were added with a fine brush and the air-brush was used for atmospherics.

Above:
Extraordinary effects of contrast can be achieved by combining gouache with watercolour techniques. Only the sky was air-brushed in this detail from FOREST KINGDOM ('The Pentateuch' 1979).

FOUR: OILS

Alla prima, grisaille, glazes and scumbles, tinting etc.. The supreme medium for both effect and durability.

My way of using oils is obviously somewhat individual, rather meticulous, perhaps even old-fashioned, so the opinions and methods I am going to describe in this chapter are in no way meant as a guide for others. This is just an account of my own personal preferences.

However there are certain basic principles emphasized here which I believe should always be observed when working in oils, especially where permanence and durability are required. Any craftsman has a duty to understand his materials and their properties. If he uses them incorrectly or in such a way that his work won't survive, then surely he is cheating not only his customer, but also posterity and his own name.

The first consideration when painting in oils is the preparation of a suitable ground on a suitable support. I prefer to work on the smooth side of hardboard prepared with several coats of Winsor & Newton's oil-based primer. The hardboard is thoroughly braced, and the back is also protected by a few coats of paint. The surface is roughened and sized before priming, then left to mature for at least half a year. I never use freshly primed boards, for the surface is too absorbent, and will not allow satisfactory 'working' of the paint once in place.

Usually I rub down the mature priming with 'wet & dry' or sandpaper. This not only removes the inevitable surface oiliness, but also makes a good 'key' to which the paint will take well. An almost glass-like smoothness may be achieved by using fine 'wet & dry' abrasive paper in a wet condition. In very small miniature work this smoothness may be useful, but for larger paintings it may well be a disadvantage, as the paint tends to 'push around' to easily.

I rarely use canvas, although its lightness is a great advantage for large paintings and the weave can give an attractive overall texture. It is an inherently unstable support and must eventually be bonded to panels anyway.

Other good supports are marine plywood and well-roughened white laminate such as Formica or Warerite, though all of these may have disadvantages too. It is well-known that any wooden support — even plywood — may eventually crack or warp, and plastic laminate is too recent an invention to have proved

Below:
In this detail from UNTO US A SON IS GIVEN (1969) most of the work was completed in a single coat. The paint on the brickwork and shutter is very thick, and had to be scraped back to the white primer before the chain, flowers etc. could be painted in.

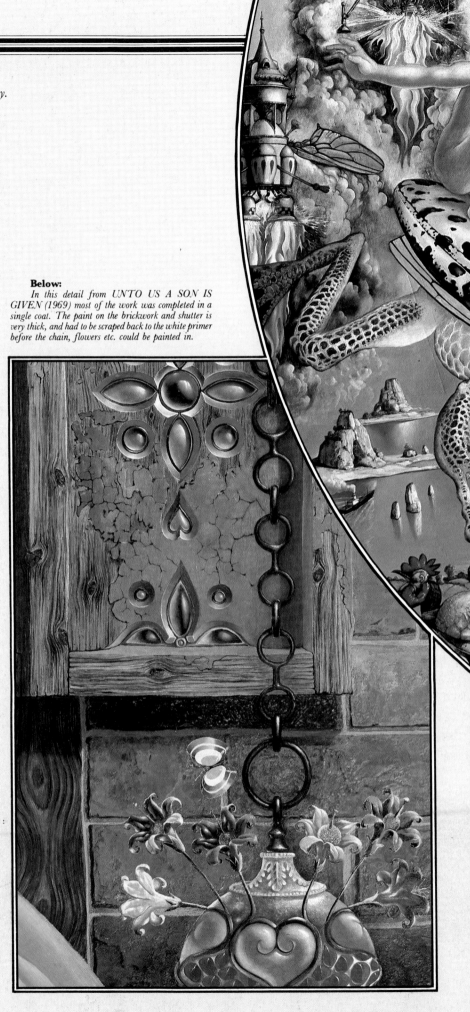

Above:
THE SUMMERHOUSE was completed in 1972, after I had learnt how to use more than one coat of oil-paint. Even so, many details in this painting — the flying frog for example — were finished in one coat (alla prima).
(Detail approximately actual size.)

Left:
Detail from HUNTING PARTY AT THE WORLD'S END (1967). Most of this early oil-painting was done in one coat. To achieve the exotic royal sleeve of emerald and scarlet it was necessary to separate the two colours with a barrier of yellow. When each colour is applied as a separate coat, even the most incompatible pigments present no problems — at least not in application.

84

Opposite page:

Unfortunately there was too little time for correct under-painting procedures when I did this sleeve painting for the Pallas album 'The Sentinel' (1983).

The basic graded sky-tone had been laid many years previously with a roller, so a satisfactorily mature ground — essential for performance — was unfortunately already to hand.

Unlike most of my work, this painting developed entirely without drawing or planning. The paints were applied extremely thinly, all the time using a small amount of Liquin, so that they would dry quickly enough to enable re-touching very soon after.

The illustration was delivered in transparency form. It was still not dry enough to transport even when the album appeared in the shops!

This page:

The painting for Mike Bat's album was commissioned in 1984. Most of the picture was given two coats of paint, though the second coat locally only consisted of adjustments here and there for contrast.

The rainbow was applied with an air-brush.

The Snark is reputed to have a fondness for bathing-machines. The device in the foreground is one of many bathing-machine ideas which I developed while developed while working on this project.

The pencil sketch for this painting is reproduced on page 39.

itself durable. Well-braced hardboard seems the safest bet.

Sketches may be traced in the usual way and very accurate drawing is possible with hard pencils, but I usually try to dispense with drawing as far as possible, because it tends to hinder the free and expressive use of paint.

The actual painting may be completed in one coat only (alla prima), but much greater depth and contrast are possible if two or more coats are applied. There are also other good reasons — which any good house-painter must also understand — for applying several thin layers of paint rather than one thick one.

All paints have their own distinctive chemical properties. It is not only the colour that varies. Some are transparent, others opaque. Different oils may be used in the grinding. The pigments themselves may even affect each other chemically and produce immediate or long-term unwanted effects.

For these reasons alone I usually choose to follow the old well-tried methods, but other factors are also important. Oil-paints nearly always undergo two fundamental changes after they have been applied. First, they tend to darken. Second, they tend to become transparent. Whenever I paint in oils I try to keep these two principles in mind, so that a colour achieved with a transparent glaze — even though the oil may darken — remains brilliant by virtue of its increasing transparency.

The underpainting (or 'grisaille') is a tonal foundation, usually opaque, made up from the cheaper 'earth' colours — umber, ochre, sienna, Indian red. I try to make this coat as accurate as possible and only as thick as is absolutely necessary.

Only a diluent is used at this stage to make the paint more workable. Genuine turpentine is best, for it enables the work to proceed almost as easily as watercolour. Oil of spike lavender is a good alternative, especially as turpentine may be degraded if stored in bright light or if bottles are left unstoppered. Though liquid, the thinned paint soon stiffens after application, and can then be worked like a buttery paste.

I often use various dry brushes to blend and manipulate the paint long after it has been applied. Though many of them are expensive sables, I am becoming increasingly adept with the new nylon brushes. Unfortunately the nylon hairs tend to become distorted, but the brushes are after all not so expensive as sables and can be thrown away more readily.

Large areas with little or no detail obviously require larger tools. Flat square nylon brushes are excellent for applying paint like this, though other brushes (sable fans etc.) may be

My obsession with the snake-tree image dates back to the mid-sixties when the above sketch was done. Not until 1972 did it appear complete on the left-hand volet of my triptych THE THOUSAND-YEAR ROUNDABOUT. At the time I was eagerly experimenting with the strange colour combinations that are made possible by using thin glazes of transparent pigment over a coloured or monochrome underpainting.

Ten years later I used the image again to illustrate my lyric THE HEDGEBANK NUN in 'Hallelujah Anyway' (1984), though this time the underpainting seemed somehow sufficient on its own and was never finished. The sky was applied months in advance with a roller and scraped back to the priming with scalpels for all subsequent work.

Above:
THE HEDGEBANK NUN herself (1983) was also left unfinished. It illustrates how raw umber and titanium white makes an excellent general underpainting, whereas green is traditionally used as a first coat when painting flesh.

Below:
for MOUNTAIN DRAGONS OF BRITISH COLUMBIA (1977-detail) I used Indian red and yellow ochre as an underpainting for the sky. The wings were underpainted in flat cadmium yellow.
The rocks and some other details were painted alla prima (in one coat).

needed for 'dry' blending afterwards.

Graded colour for skies etc. can be applied with a soft rubber roller, but if it is to be painted over, I prefer to treat it as any other ground, and allow it to mature for as long as possible. If I am impatient, I may scrape away all areas where further work is to be done, so that once again I have all the advantages of working directly on the clean white ground. This takes enormous patience, but is well worth the effort. Any colour — opaque or not — placed over another will inevitably be affected to some degree by the colour underneath. Unless the colours are compatible and enhance each oither — green on blue, perhaps — the effect is usually deadening and should be avoided, unless of course that is the effect required.

As far as possible the underpainting is warm rather than cold. Colours laid over warm browns and reds seem to glow wonderfully, for in using two coats of paint it is possible to put colours together in a way impossible when both are wet at the same time.

All colours are affected by those around them. A neutral grey for example may seem blue when it appears near red, yet the same grey may look pink when surrounded by green. This is an extreme example, but the principle always applies and is worth bearing in mind. On the other hand it is easy to become so distracted by experimental contrasts and sour discords, that the effect on the eye — though startling — may not necessarily be pleasing. Aesthetic considerations must never defer to technical fun and games.

The underpainting — or for that matter any subsequent layer of paint — is then left for a few weeks to dry and harden. The more inert the grisaille, the more stable will be the overpainting. Oil-paints in fact never reach a static point after which they cease to change, and although they will always to some degree be affected by coats of paint applied later, it is generally safe to do this after six weeks, provided the first coat is fairly thin.

Finishing is satisfying and exciting, especially after the picture has lain for so long in a frustratingly incomplete state. A difficulty I always have after leaving a piece for so long is to re-kindle my enthusiasm for the job in hand. In fact some of my underpaintings never received a top coat, and have had to be used as illustrations in their unfinished grisaille state.

Winton oil-painting medium is excellent for the finishing coat, but I have come to prefer their recently developed oil/resin medium 'Liquin', which is more controllable and dries more readily.

Glazes may be small or large. Only a tiny speck of paint may be applied to represent a leaf, but at the

The grisaille for AU SECOURS! (1980) was done mainly in raw umber, though a delicate green was used for the flesh. The main colour for the glaze on the masonry was raw sienna, though sap green and burnt umber were also used.

Such pigments as Winsor green — the very strong green used for the head-dress — must be used very sparingly indeed if they are not to kill all the colour elsewhere in the picture.

A coat of raw sienna was applied to the lace cloth before the white finishing coat — this to give it greater warmth, for whites applied thinly over darker colours tend the appear slightly blue.
(Details approximately actual size.)

THE MYSTERY OF FLIGHT (1980).

Blue light reflected from the sea was added here as a scumble (overpainting in thin light colours) as was the effect of white water running slowly over the sand. The raw sienna underlying the girl's dress does much to improve the quality of the white. Tiny details — the farmer and the ship — were added very quickly without re-touching.

Indian red makes a very good underpainting for green — here mainly sap green — in THE CORN FAIRY (1981), another illustration for 'Hallelujah Anyway'. Liquin oleo-resin medium is very easy to control in fine detail. It dries quickly too.

Opposite page:
Three stages in the development of TRES-PASSERS WILL BE WELCOME (1980). At least six weeks passed between the underpainting and stage two. This is an essential precaution to ensure that the first coat is as inert as possible.

Above and below:
Two stages of ALICIA AND SARAH (1980). This picture was, as can be readily seen, almost completed in one coat. Except for the lilies and the blue scumbling of ripples on the water, the second coat simply consisted of small touches here and there to adjust contrast, tone etc.. Any colour difference perceptible in the sky area is attributable to photographic variables rather than to extra work from myself.

A pale pink, fading to pale ochre at the horizon, was applied as underpainting for the sky in THE ELVEN DRUMMER (1980). Sea and cliffs were also underpainted in warm reds and browns. This gave an excellent base for blue glazes and misty scumbles.

The Sun's rays were applied with the aid of a mahlstick mounted on a pivot to ensure that they radiated correctly.

Opposite page:
Much of the careful blending I did in the grisaille of COME HITHER FROM THE RAIN (1980) proved to be a waste of time. Most of it was eventually covered by storm clouds.

This is one of those occasions where I think I prefer the grisaille to the finished picture.

other extreme a thin glaze of very dilute paint may be used to cover the whole picture with a unifying tint. Thick glazes are not very effective, and it must always be remembered that nothing can be concealed forever by a thick coat of what is basically a transparent pigment. Hundreds of examples can be seen in old paintings where for instance a tree-trunk becomes translucent as it crosses a bright patch of sky. This is called a 'pentimento' and can ruin otherwise good work.

Liquin dries very quickly — touch-dry often within a day — which enables me to reinforce the colour or to make other adjustments as the paints get progressively tackier. Once properly dry however, it should not be over-painted for at least a few days, and then only with very thin glazes.

To achieve very fine detail it is obviously necessary to use very fine brushes. These are all expensive, especially the sables, and will last longer if kept scrupulously clean. Rinsing in white spirit is usually enough, but if brushes are to be left unused for any length of time, it is advisable to wash them in soap and warm water. Points can be restored by putting the brush in your mouth and then allowing the slightly cohesive saliva to dry.

A brush-bath — though rather expensive to buy — is a very good investment if you want to avoid the chore of cleaning brushes too often. The brushes simply hang in white spirit till required. Needless to say, they should not be left like this for more than a day or two.

Brushwork itself is a very personal thing. Every painter discovers his own manner. When working on very fine detail I have developed the habit of slightly twisting the brush with each stroke. This tends to keep the point tight by preventing the brush from fanning. However, when working with a dry brush to blend or adjust paint that has already been applied, it is often necessary to do the exact opposite — to push the hairs apart with the fingers so that they do indeed form a fan. Old sables are best for this. Very delicate touches with the tips of the hairs can make the most delicate blendings. Remove paint from the brush periodically, otherwise the work becomes progressively more gross. A properly made fan-brush is only useful for large areas, but the method is the same.

'Scumbling' — the opposite of glazing — is done with opaque colours. It is advisable to add raw sienna or some other warm pigment when working white scumbles, for any white paint tends to appear blue when placed over a dark ground.

To achieve great detail I often apply thick touches of this white — painting not really with the brush but

93

Home-made equipment:

A fixed rag (1) is useful for wiping the brush when only one hand is free. Horizontal and vertical brush-stands (2) keep dirty brushes under control on the work-table. My 'library' palette (3) has a place for every colour I use. Tube paints are sometimes hard to distinguish on the palette, so I always put them out in the same order so that I know where to look. The smallest palette just consists of a Formica cut-out. The larger ones are mounted on plywood. Various bridges (4) of different sizes (and depths) are a useful way of supporting the arms and wrists when painting with the work flat on a table. The mahlstick (5) can be fixed to the bench with double-sided tape to provide a radial guide when painting sunbeams etc.. A conventional mahlstick (6) is easily made from bamboo and a wad of cotton wool. Useful reversible dippers (7) can be made by sticking sea-shells back to back with resin filler. A friend made the ceramic versions also shown here.

Above:
Conventional tools:

A sponge (1) is useful for applying thin uniform glazes over large areas. The palette-knife (2) can also sometimes be used more effectively than a brush to cover large areas, but I personally prefer its use to be undetectable in the finished work. A ready-made fan brush (3) or an old sable pushed into a fan-shape with the fingers are essential tools for blending. Old and new fine nylon brushes (4) are good for detailed work, but a thin sable with very few hairs left (5) is useful for putting in stiff dabs of paint where a new brush would be too thick. A flat nylon brush (6) is excellent for covering large areas and for glazing. Scalpels (7) are used to scrape back to the white priming when overpainting would be too risky. Tweezers (8) are essential for removing stray dust and hairs while the work is in progress. Dusting brushes (9) remove dust before the day's work begins.

Below:
Detail from GLASS (1979).

This is a good example of how oil-painting may be used as a top-coat over watercolour. The background was air-brushed in gouache.

virtually with a tiny lump of stiff paint hanging from the end. These tiny impastos tend to grab the light and make the work more three-dimensional. Adjustments may be made to these with another (dry) brush to blend them in or even to remove them entirely.

This is one of the great advantages of working in oils — especially in two coats — there are very few mistakes that cannot be totally removed before they dry. Dab the offending area with a brush loaded with turpentine; lift the paint by repeatedly drinking it up with a dry brush and wiping this on a rag.

The importance of rags cannot be over-emphasized. I periodically prepare a large stock in various sizes from old sheets, shirts etc.. I always keep a tiny (100 millimetre) square to hand for cleaning my smallest brushes as I paint, but obviously a good supply of larger rags is needed for big brushes, palettes etc.. When cleaning small brushes repeatedly during work it is sometimes helpful to have a fixed rag pinned down near at hand to wipe them on, thus leaving the other hand free to hold the palette or whatever.

This is one of the many home-made gadgets I have accumulated in my studio over the years. A brush-stand for example (horizontal or vertical) is very useful to keep loaded brushes under control and apart from each other.

White Formica is undoubtedly the best material for home-made palettes. Not only is it light and durable, but the colours are easily assessed against its pure white background. I use various sizes according to the scale of the work, but I am usually happiest with a small piece about 150×100 millimetres which I clean repeatedly. As a receptacle for the day's supply of colours I have another home-made palette on which I always lay out the pigments in a particular order, because dabs of tube-paint can sometimes be hard to identify.

I usually work at a table with the painting in a horizontal position, so I have had to make various 'bridges' etc. to support my hand and elbows. These also help to protect the work from dust and from accidental damage. When working vertical at the easel however, a home-made mahlstick is useful for supporting the hand. A simple development of this — a mahlstick fixed at the top with an adjustable pivot — makes a good guide when painting radiating sunbeams.

I also used to make my own reversible dippers (for diluents, media and liquid paint) from limpet or cockle shells. Recently however I have had some specially made in ceramic to my own 'limpet' design. The virtues of a conical receptacle for liquids are obvious, but no such thing seems to be

Above:
REQUIESCAT POLLY (1983), shown here only in part, illustrates how readily oils may be used as a glaze over a pen and ink drawing. Correct mounting and preparation of the drawing are essential.

Right:
In WHERE THE SEA-FAUNS LIE (1983) all the colour is put on very thinly. This ensures that sufficient light can be reflected from the white surface back through the paint layer to give the pigment its optimum effect.

Above:

Detail from NO PLACE FOR THE NAIVE (1981). Etchings — provided the proof is pulled on fine quality board and properly prepared and dried — make a superb base for oil-tinting. The paint seems to fall into place in pools of colour, being slightly restricted in its movement by the relief of the intaglio line.

Below:

A cartouche from 'Hallelujah Anyway' (1980). This is also an etching tinted with oils. The motto reads: 'Do not allow art to become a labour; let's not forget the beauty of reality.'

available in the shops.

I have also made some modest innovations in the technical side of oil-painting. I have already described the processes of painting in oils over ink drawings and etchings, but it is also possible to do the same thing on top of watercolour, as long as the method used prevents the oil-paint from coming into contact with the paper. I described this technique in the previous chapter. The only difference with watercolour is that any mattness or opacity in the first coat tends to disappear as the glaze is applied. The effect has to be seen to be appreciated, but it is easily rectified in the oil-paint stage of the work.

It is also possible to apply oils with an air-brush. The paint should of course be extremely dilute — almost watery — otherwise it will give a very pronounced granular texture. I use genuine turpentine for this, adding a small quantity of Liquin to ensure that the rather delicate paint-film is properly bound. Once again, the advantages of oils over other media become evident, for any errors are easily corrected simply by gently wiping them off and starting again.

To paint a rainbow with an air-brush it is useful to have some sort of template mounted at least 20 millimetres above the picture surface. For this I attach a piece of cardboard to a bridge; the card is already drawn up with a series of concentric arcs. For each colour I cut away another curved strip, so that the rainbow can be part of a perfect circle. This method is however only possible on a fairly large scale, and when painting small rainbows I simply apply the colours one at a time with a clean brush, then blend them with a dry fanned sable. I always add a little white and raw sienna to the tints, otherwise they are not sufficiently light and opaque: the rainbow must if possible appear lighter than its background.

There are very few other occasions when an air-brush is useful in oils, simply because blending and controlling subtle scumbles and glazes is extremely easy anyway in this medium, and conventional brushes will probably do the job far better.

The methods of applying paint are of course almost unlimited. I use not only brushes and knives, but also rags, sponges — even my fingers — though this may not be apparent from the final result, because quantities of paint are often so small as to be almost unnoticeable.

Interesting effects, though of limited use, may be achieved by dripping very dilute paint onto an already-painted (wet) surfce. The turpentine in the dilute paint will slowly spread through, leaving strange blossom-like forms, or, if taken to extremes, will produce an effect reminiscent of marbling.

I have already described how oils may be applied with a roller for graded tonal skies etc.. This method can also be used in the final coat to apply misty effects or even rainbows. The effects are similar to those possible with an air-brush, but the process is far quicker and easier.

Techniques develop. Methods multiply. New tools and equipment make new possibilities. Yet somehow the best results still seem to come from the simplest, most traditional processes. Perhaps this is because — uncorrupted by technical considerations — the original idea comes through, spontaneous, immediate, naïve — like the exclamation of an emotion before it has been translated into words.

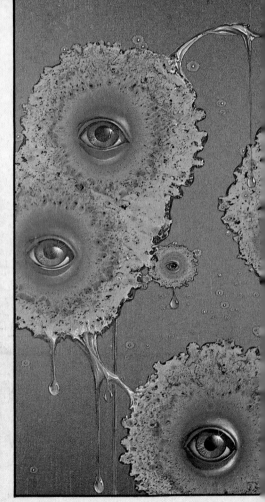

Left:
Detail from HORTUS CONCLUSUS (1982). Much of the complex underpainting was scraped back to the priming to permit the waterfall to extend much further across this painting than originally intended.

Stiff white highlights were applied with an ancient sable containing only three or four hairs. These touches were then blended in with a larger fanned brush.

Below left:
Detail from DRY LAND (from 'The Pentateuch' 1979). Stiff white highlights give quite convincing substance to sea and rocks in this tiny corner of an uncharacteristically conventional landscape.

Right:
An air-brush was used to provide the rainbow in this unused record label (1983). Oils should be diluted with turpentine for this, but a little medium should also be added so that the pigment is sufficiently bound, and does not simply rest on the surface like a powder.

Below:
In this illustration for 'The Pentateuch' (1979) droplets of turpentine were allowed to eat away into the wet paint. The eyes etc. were painted in later when this was dry. Both the background and the rainbow were applied with a soft rubber roller.

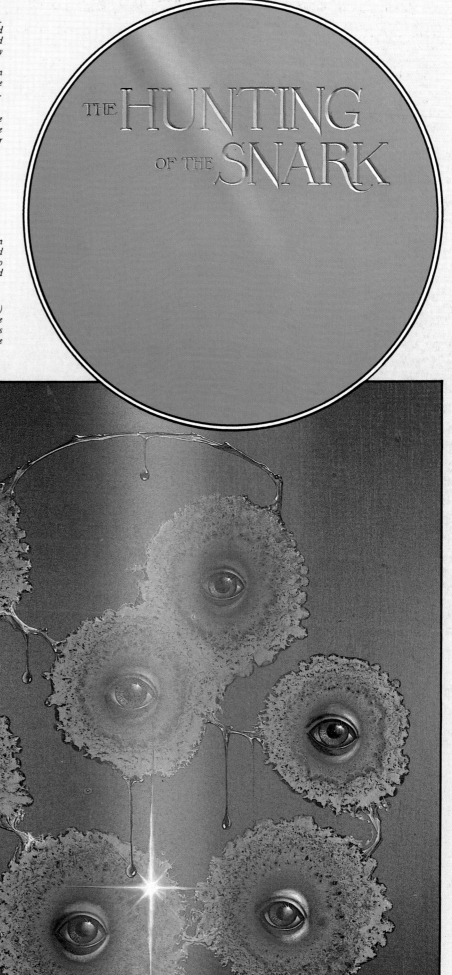

Above:

This bizarre creature from *MIASMA GENERATOR (1979)* took shape as I painted it. I had no idea what I was doing, but I did know what message I wanted to convey with that pathetic accusing eye.

The rainbow/lightning, a symbol of the broken covenant between God and man, was put on with brushes and blended with a dry fan improvised from an old sable.

Above:

For *DERELICTUS IN CAELO (detail 1978)* white paint overlies a predominantly pink and grey underpainting. All surface details of the planet were achieved in the second coat.

Below:

Detail from *THE MILK ROBBERS (1982)*. Stiff touches of yellow in the grass show how texture may be used to give greater realism. Under slightly raking light the effect is of course even greater.

TINKER SAYS GOODBYE (1977) This tiny painting (considerably enlarged in the above detail) is a good example of how readily oil-paint may be persuaded to produce accurate work — provided the correct media and brushes are used. Like many of my oil-paintings, this one was done on a carefully prepared hardboard panel primed well in advance.

A semi-photographic process.

In the late seventies I thought I had invented this word 'tomograph', until I discovered that the medical profession had long been using it to describe a particular type of scan. Made up from the Greek words for 'cut' and 'drawing', it seemed the ideal name for a process I have used in which painted cut-outs are photographed in 'real' (that is non-painted) locations. The intention is to enable the painted image to escape into the real world, thereby creating strange interactions and encounters that — hopefully — baffle the eye.

This is by no means an original technique; it has been in common use in 'trick' photography for years. However, in my case it is possibly the first time a painter — rather than a photographer — has made use of it. The origins of the tomograph in my own work date back to about 1979 when I first started work on 'Hallelujah Anyway'. One of my lyrics which I illustrated for this book required an accurate perspective drawing of a cut-out representing a 'damsel in distress'. This presented no great problem — the foreshortening could be achieved by squaring up the sketch and re-drawing it on a perspective grid — but I made a card cut-out from the sketch anyway, just to see how it would look in practice.

Cutting it out from card was very difficult, and the result was most fragile and unsatisfactory, but it encouraged me to look for an alternative material that would be better than card.

When properly abraded and primed, copper is an excellent support for oil-paints, but cutting it out with a fine-tooth fret-saw and files is a slow and laborious task. The roughened metal must be given at least two coats of oil-based primer several months before use. Unfortunately this means that the copper is primed *before* cutting — a difficult task which is almost impossible without damaging the priming along the edge of the cut. Not only is it very hard work to cut copper accurately, but the metal also presents other problems. Very fine delicate forms are impossible to achieve without days of careful labour. A copper cut-out is heavy, and therefore difficult to support in a photographic set-up. Most important of all, copper is very expensive, and cut-outs leave a lot of waste.

What I was looking for then was a

Above:
For my recent exhibition in Folkestone (1985) I mounted all my tomographs in a total of ten glazed cases. Although these painted cut-outs were of course only intended for use in photographic images, the original laminate models make an interesting display.

Opposite page:
From a complex studio set-up, with tank, painted back-drop, suspended lighting and heavy props, came this curious image SECOND MONDAY, symbolic of ecological disaster. The distance from lens to back-drop was approximately two metres.

102

For me the tomograph originates in my early work for 'Hallelujah Anyway'. This Madonna and child (for Neddy and Rosie 1982) consists of many separate elements.

The central figures are cut from primed copper sheet and mounted in a groove within the box frame. The background landscape painting fits onto the main frame with screws, but has an aperture to allow access to the batteries which power the lighting circuit.

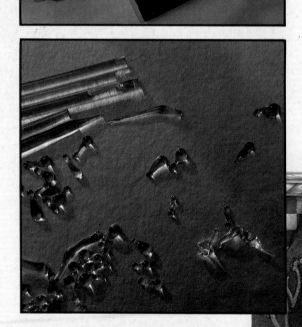

The front consists of plywood coated many times with enamels and rubbed down with wet & dry. Beads made from glass rod drawn and melted over a gas flame provide extra embellishments for the doors.

My daughter Rosie, for whom this was made as a Christmas gift and whose toy donkey also figures in the background, devotedly closes the doors every night before sleeping.

104

THE FORGET-ME-NOT GARDENER
also had a built-in lighting circuit, but an unfortunate
leak from the batteries did considerable damage to the
back of the copper cut-out, so I removed the circuit. To
photograph it satisfactorily I had to mount it with the
right-hand sides of the box removed so that a good raking
light could illuminate the background.

Small decorative hinges for the doors were made by
cutting down conventional ones, and pieces of scrap brass
were adapted for knobs etc.. White impressions and
sockets for beads were made with the aid of a countersink
bit.

The whole ensemble is coated with wax varnish
for protection against tarnish etc..

105

substance strong enough to be cut with a fret or piercing saw, light, cheap and relatively stable. The answer proved to be white plastic laminate, 'Formica' or 'Warerite', which when properly prepared and supported, seems to be the perfect material for this purpose.

Careful preparation of the white surface is very important. When newly bought, this laminate is very smooth — almost glossy; it may also be greasy or dirty. It must be cleaned and made thoroughly matt by rubbing with fairly coarse wet & dry abrasive paper. It is advisable to prepare a large quantity at a time, for this job makes a lot of very fine white dust which seems to get everywhere. All dust residues should be carefully removed from the surface with a soft cloth.

I always wear thin cotton gloves when abrading, cutting or drawing on laminate. This is the simplest way to ensure that the surface remains free of any grease or dirt which may stop the paint from taking properly. A stock of prepared sheets may be wrapped in paper or stored in envelopes.

When using only oil-paints it seems unnecessary to paint the back of the laminate. I have little experience of other media, but when using acrylic as an underpainting, shrinkage of the paint may cause warping. I have only come across this once, and if the back of the cut-out is properly reinforced with struts of wood, there should be no appreciable distortion anyway.

Drawing on laminate is not the same as drawing on paper or board. Although the sketch is easily traced in the normal way, very hard (9H and 5H) pencils are needed for the final drawing. Sadly, the surface is so hard that free, expressive work is impossible, but the real purpose of the drawing is only to establish the exact outline of the subject ready for cutting.

For some tomographs (where strength is more important than complexity) I use a laminate approximately 1 millimetre in thickness, but for many subjects a .5 millimetre sheet is much better, because the thinner the laminate, the quicker it is to cut. It is also lighter and therefore easier to support for shooting.

A firm board with a key-hole slot (such as is usually used in fret-saw work) enables easy control of the laminate while it is cut. It is safer to keep waste material in place with Sellotape until the whole cut is finished; this helps to protect delicate protuberances from accidental damage.

The main outline is best started from a small drilled hole; this is of course also necessary when taking a shaped piece from the middle of a cut-out. I always do all necessary drilling before I start sawing; this saves the trouble of changing tools too often.

The cutting is done with a piercing saw or fret-saw fitted with

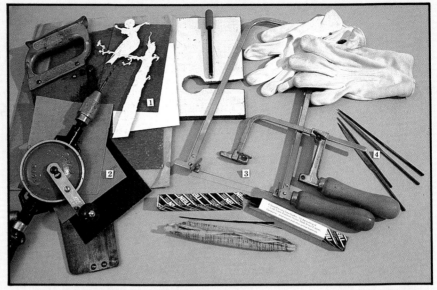

Cutting a tomograph:
Formica plastic laminate (1) is the perfect support when rubbed down thoroughly with wet & dry abrasive paper (2). When cutting with a piercing saw (3) or smoothing the edges with a file (4), it is advisable to wear soft gloves to avoid making the delicate surface greasy.

Below:
This cut-out PERI-MALVIS is made from .5mm. laminate. Thicker Formica would have taken far longer to cut, but would of course have been a lot stronger.

Two banks of real vegetation were used on this shot, separated by about half a metre. The painted backboard — nicely out of focus — is hung about the same distance beyond that. The tomograph is mounted very simply — with screws to a cross-member at the top.

Left:

When cutting a tomograph it is advisable to use a proper fret-work bench. This enables the delicate plastic to be fully supported. Blades should be fitted so that the teeth point down towards the workpiece, and all cuts should be bevelled so as to be invisible to the camera.

Right:

The back must be reinforced with small strips of wood, especially if the cut-out is a large one. It is preferable if all this work is done to the same thickness so that the cut-out may lie flat while it is being painted.

Below:

THE JAG-JAW BEASTIE, complete with genuine glass eye, about to wreak havoc with the children's toys. Tongue, jaw and all vertebrae are fully articulated with very thin bolts.

A red spotlight was used in this shot to give extra colour to a brown back-drop.

Tomographs are more manageable when stuck to pieces of cardboard with double-sided tape. Various bridges are extremely useful for resting the hand or wrist while painting. The first coat should be diluted only with thinners (turpentine or lavender oil) and use only warm monochrome pigments. Only in the second coat are thin, strong colours applied, this time using a medium such as Liquin.

Below:

THE APPLE GLUTTON in a fairly simple studio shot. The branches are attached to the bench with G-cramps and crocodile clips. Small droplets of water were added with a hypodermic syringe. The background is of course painted. The same boards were re-painted over and over again to provide many different skies, seas etc. .

108

Above:
Genuine glass eyes are useful for tomographs. They can be fitted into sockets so that they may be moved. Many of my tomographs have alternative, moving or interchangeable parts.

Below:
The only 'real' element in this illustration, NEAR DURGAN — AUGUST, is the rock. The landscape was drawn very broadly with watercolours and oil-crayons. Because the background is mounted about half a metre beyond the cut-out, it is sufficiently out of focus not to be immediately recognisable as faked.

extremely fine blades. The finer the blade the greater its capacity to turn and make reversed lines. The work should proceed very carefully and gently. Any hurry or clumsiness will probably break the blade, and re-threading a new blade takes time. In any event the blades last only a very short time, and need to be bought by the box rather than by the packet. Always use the blade with the teeth pointing down towards the white surface of the piece.

The cut must be made at an angle so that the edge of the cut-out is bevelled from behind and thus not visible to a camera lens placed directly in front of it. I always saw around a cut-out in the same anti-clockwise direction, so that making a bevelled cut is now an unconscious habit.

When all the sawing is done, the edges and corners are gently filed to eliminate tooth-marks etc.. I always make sure that the work-piece is well supported, and just like sawing, all filing is done downwards so as not to spoil the edge. Very tight inside corners may be sharpened with a scalpel to eliminate curves where the saw has visibly changed direction.

Small reinforcing pieces of wood stuck on the back of the cut-out will not only prevent warping, but also enable it to be easily handled and supported. On especially narrow parts it may be necessary to bevel or otherwise modify these bracings so that they will not be visible to the camera.

Before painting begins it is useful to stick the tomograph to a piece of card with double-sided tape. Again, this enables it to be easily manipulated during the process, and also helps to protect it during storage.

A simple cut-out is often quite convincing without any further additions, but since I started making tomographs I have experimented with all kinds of extras.

One interesting variation is to attach several levels together and to bridge these levels with resin filler. I use this method for example when I need to fit a glass eye into a recessed socket. In this case it is usually also necessary to incorporate eyelids made from folded cloth. Filler and cloth are both of course primed before being painted on.

A simple cut-out may also be given alternative variants by attaching movable or interchangeable parts. A nut and bolt soldered to a disc of copper sheet makes a good pivot. It can be stuck to the back of a movable limb or wing and passed through a hole in the main body of the cut-out.

Alternative positions — open and closed beaks etc. — are readily achieved with separate pieces fitted into slots. Care must be taken to cover any joints from behind so that light does not show through. Black Plasti-

Below:

SAINT ANTHONY'S PULPIT also consists of several moving and interchangeable parts. Not only that — the little gothic window can be lit up on a circuit powered by a torch battery.

Very thin cut-outs must obviously be handled very carefully, though it is possible to make quick strong repairs with Superglue and extra reinforcements on the back.

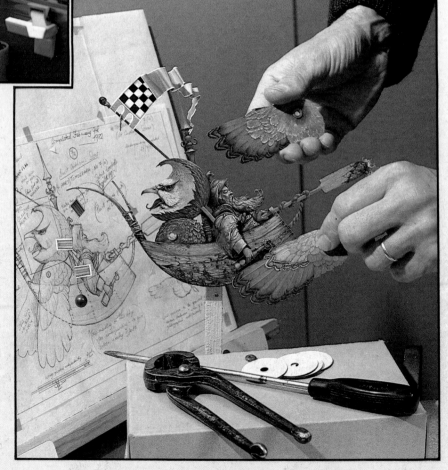

Above:

THE NEW MESSIAH'S SKY-BOAT has interchangeable parts that fit into slots. The whole tomograph consists of more than a dozen separate parts, so that a huge variety of variants may be produced.

It is securely screwed to a wooden batten which for the shot was invisible to the camera behind one of the wings.

Right:

Slots and pivots are just two ways to provide tomographs with variants. Non-painted elements may also be added — the possibilities are endless.

Opposite page:

St. Anthony preaches to the fishes in this very complex studio shot. The water-level conceals the base-mounting of the saint's pulpit, which has a lighting circuit wired to a torch battery. Heavy rocks were used as props to provide a middle ground. The background, complete with black nimbus, was of course painted. The nimbus was done with an air-brush, using ever smaller discs of card as masks.

Above:

Simple shots requiring few props may very easily be taken out of doors, though the wind can be a problem. Invisible to the camera lens, all rods and clips used to support the cut-out are concealed behind it.

Below:

All kinds of rods, clips, screw-plates, some jointed, some pliable, were evolved to support the cut-outs. Double-sided tape, Plasticine and adhesive putty are all very useful.

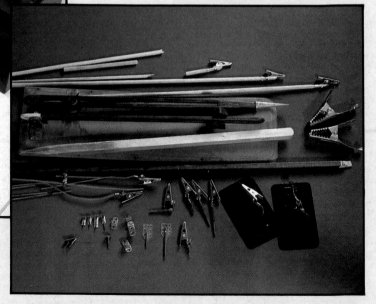

Though rather heavy, an MPP 5"×4" camera is an extremely versatile piece of equipment. A firm tripod is essential for steady shots, but a satisfactory cheap version can be improvised from a sketching easel. Sheet film is loaded into 'dark-slides' either in a dark-room or a dark-box.

Above:

A simple outdoor shot.

The cut-outs have been simply placed on the ground and propped up so that they are parallel with the back-plate of the camera. The cut edge, if bevelled, should not be visible. Feathers, wire and beads help to give extra realism.

Below:

For ground-level shots like the one above, I made up a contraption which made an effective adjustable support both for the MPP and for my 35mm. camera. This is also useful for table-top set-ups in the studio.

Above:

Boojum/photographer. A sketch tinted with watercolour for the project 'The Hunting of the Snark' (1983).

cine is useful for this, but tape is a good alternative.

One weakness of the cut-out tends to be the outline itself, for if the shape is too simple it may be too readily discernible. Various extraneous additions are possible — hair stuck in filler, beads set into sockets, string, chains, feathers etc.. Anything that leads to greater ambiguity and confusion will make the tomograph more realistic.

Strangely enough however, such additions are often unnecessary if the cutting and photography are well done, and painted details may even be more convincing than real items incorporated in the work.

Painting proceeds as usual with oils, though the laminate is relatively unabsorbent and has a very different 'feel' from other surfaces. If speed is necessary, the first coat may be applied in acrylic, though I find 'oil on oil' far more satisfactory in the long run.

The final coat — of transparent glazes and opaque scumbles — is obviously crucial. The finish must be neither too glossy nor too matt. A high gloss may reflect extraneous light and destroy the depth of dark areas, while matt tones never give so much contrast as slightly glossy ones.

It is sometimes very effective to render small highlights with touches of thick impasto so that they seem to glow in a raking light. This does not always make the image more beautiful, especially after it has been through the rigours of the printing process, but when used sparingly it can make things more realistic.

Photographing the tomograph can be exciting and rewarding, but more often than not it is difficult and frustrating. It all depends on whether you are looking for a happy chance or trying to replicate an image already in the mind. The process itself can be as simple or as complex as you care to make it, but the most effective results are often achieved in the simplest way, and a very difficult studio shot, with all kinds of multi-layered 'props', can often prove to be a complete waste of time. Many of my most effective shots have in fact been the result of a process of trial and error in which almost all non-painted elements have eventually been left out. In other words the finished result is a painting in all but name, a multi-layered image in which the only advantage provided photographically has been the inimitable blurring of close foreground or distant background.

To support a tomograph effectively while it is being photographed presents many problems. All manner of contrivances — wires, pivots, clamps, clips, pins, screwplates etc. — were needed to produce the pictures in 'Hallelujah Anyway'.

It is of course essential that all

Beads, feathers, string, wire, chains — even hair — can be incorporated into the tomograph design in order to give it more realism. The mother and child in this tomograph are shown in two alternative poses which simply fit into a slot. Small lengths of bamboo set in resin filler made good sockets for the feathers.

During painting, each component of the model was mounted separately on a small piece of card, so that all parts of the cut-out could be reached easily with the brush. Not until it was finally assembled weeks later did I really know how it would look.

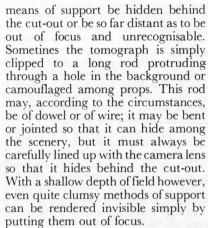

Above:

To support a small, light cut-out a glass screen may be used. The cut-out is fixed with double-sided tape. Anything very light-coloured is however liable to be reflected in the glass: even the camera lens may appear on the shot as a blurred circle. To avoid this, an adjustable black screen can be improvised, through which the camera can peep.

Below:

In this shot, DANDELION TIME, the tomograph is supported behind the glass screen on a jointed rod. Each seed was stuck to the glass with Superglue.

Even in this carefully planned shot (using a black screen) there is a fault: the lower dandelion flower is reflected in the glass.

The graded background was achieved by directing a spotlight at part of a blue-grey mounting board.

means of support be hidden behind the cut-out or be so far distant as to be out of focus and unrecognisable. Sometines the tomograph is simply clipped to a long rod protruding through a hole in the background or camouflaged among props. This rod may, according to the circumstances, be of dowel or of wire; it may be bent or jointed so that it can hide among the scenery, but it must always be carefully lined up with the camera lens so that it hides behind the cut-out. With a shallow depth of field however, even quite clumsy methods of support can be rendered invisible simply by putting them out of focus.

For supporting cut-outs in outdoor vegetation I had to make various green-camouflaged contrivances, and for work in water the gadgetry had to be painted black so that it would not be visible through reflections on the surface. Some of these were used just for one shot and may never be needed again.

Free-flying cut-outs must obviously be as light as possible, and all fittings either rigid or at least stable. Vibration from a wooden floor can be a problem in the studio, especially in long exposures, but outdoors the biggest problem is undoubtedly the wind.

The wind can also be a nuisance when cut-outs (and to some extent props) are stuck to a sheet of glass, but here problems may also arise with reflections. Not only the bevelled edge of the cut-out, but also light or brightly-lit props and even the camera itself, may be visible reflected in the glass.

The camera at least can be concealed behind an adjustable black screen with a hole cut in it, but it is very difficult to avoid other reflections.

The cut-out or props (flowers etc.) may be stuck to the glass with double-sided tape or with glue. This can be risky, as no method of sticking is totally reliable, and it can be disastrous when a cut-out crashes to the ground. Not only that — if the glue is too effective, then it may be impossible to remove the cut-out without damage.

It is also possible, though in my experience not very pleasing, to paint directly on the glass as well, for example to depict spray or water flying between layers of cut-outs. I have also experimented with marbling on sheets of glass to be used in this way, but once again the results hardly justified the effort involved, and would have been more easily achieved by conventional painting methods.

The camera I use for all this work is an old 5″×4″ MPP with the old-fashioned bellows and black hood. Each sheet of transparency film is loaded in total darkness into a 'dark-slide' which is slotted into the back of the camera. To do this I use a home-

Right:

An outdoor shot in which a glass screen has been used to support the tomograph. On this occasion the cut-out had no reinforcing struts on the back, which meant that it could be stuck down flat against the glass to avoid unwanted reflections. The real-life butterfly (a dead one naturally) was also stuck to the glass with double-sided tape.

This example shows very well how a background may be effectively blurred by using a comparatively large lens aperture.

Opposite page:

This cut-out of SAINT ANTHONY AND THE BARGEE BIRD was carefully mounted in a tank of water.

The water is only about 50mm. deep, and black polythene helps to prevent the support being visible.

A spray mister is useful for keeping vegetation fresh when set-ups like this have to remain under the hot lights for long periods.

Above:

In this studio set-up the bird was fixed to the glass screen, as were the fragments of peanuts.

The string of nuts was in fact mounted on wire and the whole assemblage photographed on its side, so that gravity would give the effect of wind fluttering the twine.

Left:

Another studio shot illustrating the use of the glass screen. Close examination reveals some unfortunate tonal variations in the background where bright objects behind the camera are reflected. This shot was made before I had improvised the black screen to prevent this sort of thing.

Opposite page:

In this studio shot the board background is pierced with pin-pricks, so that the light from a single bulb and a sheet of aluminium foil may imitate starlight.

An 8-point star filter was used to enhance the effect.

The small light in the 'pulpit' is powered by a torch battery.

116

made dark-box, which for me proved easier than trying to make a whole room light-proof. A plate-camera like this is a heavy piece of equipment and almost always needs a good tripod, for to get a workable depth of field in studio shots, exposures of many seconds' duration are usually required.

For situations very nearly at ground level however, I was forced to make a special support for the camera myself. My design can also be used with a 35 millimetre camera.

Far less equipment is needed of course if the shots are to be taken outdoors in daylight. I have had some excellent results simply with a hand-held 35 millimetre SLR, but to have total control of the image, I found that most of my shots had to be taken in the studio.

This not only enabled more layers to be used in the shot, but also opened the door to all manner of exciting methods and techniques. However I think I sometimes allowed the set-up to get rather out of hand. A cluttered studio is difficult to work in, and as I said before, there eventually comes a point at which conventional methods would certainly mean less hard work and probably more effective results too.

Here is a particularly cumbersome set-up, which I shall describe layer by layer:

First comes the camera and tripod. These have to be quite close to the subject, because most of my tomographs are, by nature of the subject-matter, rather tiny. The camera of course sees only a triangular area in front of it, so the space immediately before the lens offers very little scope for detail. However, nice blurrings can be achieved if for example foliage is mounted directly in front of the lens to give the impression that the main subject is glimpsed beyond or through some unspecified foreground.

To represent water and the beautiful symmetry of reflections, I used a 1×1.5 metre, almost triangular tank, which consisted of a shallow (60 millimetre) box lined with black polythene. Stones, sand, seaweed etc. were placed in this, and for some of my shots the combined weight of all the props was quite a strain on the work-bench that supported it all.

Cut-outs may be supported above the water or partially submerged to maximise the effects of reflections. This wonderful reflectivity can provide other head-aches of course, for it makes it even more difficult to conceal rod supports behind the cut-outs. Although the tomographs and oil-paints are of course waterproof, I never leave the pieces in the tank any longer than necessary, and I always take great care to dry them thoroughly afterwards. I am convinced that the paint will be

Above:
Roughly painted card rocks conceal rod mountings for these two mermaid cut-outs. The painted back-drop is almost too well-focussed for realism.
The sunbeams are simulated by shining a spotlight through slashed card mounted very close to the bulb.

Below:
Curious lighting effects may be achieved by using a star filter (here a 4-point) when shooting bright light in a pierced back-drop.
The direction of the rays is adjusted simply by rotating the filter in its housing.

Left:

A studio shot may be very complex indeed, though not necessarily with proportionately better results. There comes a point where conventional painting methods would produce similar effects more easily and perhaps more acceptably.

Props can be very troublesome, especially where water and vegetation are involved. In marine subjects, rocks etc. tend to get very smelly in only 24 hours, and vegetation, unless properly mounted in Oasis, obviously tends to suffer under the heat of the studio lights.

Below:

Here is a tomograph shown in two very different locations.

The shallow depth of field gives good realism in the shot with the poppy seed-heads, though in the other photograph a good effect of cast shadow is seen to integrate the cut-out possibly more effectively in its location.

For both of these shots the cut-out was supported by a long horizontal dowel joined at the far end to a vertical rod thrust into the soil.

The photograph on the right is a studio location.

undermined and peel off if left in the water for too long, though fortunately nothing like that has so far happened.

To support vegetation in a set-up the ideal solution is often that porous green substance sold to flower-arrangers under the brand-name of 'Oasis'. Large branches and twigs on the other hand must be held in place with clamps, screws and so on, provided the work is done before the heat from the studio lights causes the vegetation to wilt.

Beyond the subject itself will be a painted or plain back-drop. I painted most of my skies on large sheets of mounting board. These are placed on my easel at a distance appropriate to the degree of soft focus required for the shot. Smoke, rays of light, rainbows, haloes etc. may be painted quite roughly on the background, yet — because they are blurred — look quite convincing on the transparency.

The back-drop may also be pierced in various ways to allow light to pass through. Fire, lightning, star-light — even the sun — may be quite effectively represented by holes, tears etc. made in the board. Behind this are hung various light-sources, plain or coloured according to requirements. It helps if aluminium foil is scrumpled up and hung behind the lights to reflect light through holes that are not immediately in front of a bulb. Another method of providing light is to wire up small torch bulbs in apertures in the cut-outs. The wiring is concealed in the scenery or under the water.

Props are limitless — rotten wood, sand, moss, bark — almost anything seems to have a use in this process. While working on 'Hallelujah Anyway' my studio got more like a tip every day, and was infested with all sorts of insects that inhabited my various buckets and troughs of moss, lichen etc.. In fact one shot I did would have been totally ruined if I had not spotted a wood-louse posing unconcernedly on a crucial part of the tomograph.

Anything that does not move can be used in the set-up — or anything that moves only slowly. An exposure of about half a second is about the limit for snails, but I have been able to include bees, butterflies etc. in my shots by the simple expedient of using only dead ones.

Plans to bait outdoor set-ups in order to bring about interesting confrontations between live and fictitious beasts have so far yielded no satisfactory results. I suspect that the final result would probably rarely be worth the effort.

The studio undoubtedly offers a more controlled, more predictable situation. Controllable lighting is one aspect of studio work not to be under-estimated. Not only is it reliable and adjustable, but very interesting effects can be produced by using spotlights

Right:
This anthropomorphic blue-tit perches on the edge of the milk bottle with the help of small lengths of wire fixed to its legs with Superglue. The only other painted element in this composition is the back-drop.

It was not essential for this to be a studio shot, but having complete control of the lighting did mean that I could be sure of a satisfactory cast shadow of the bird's tail.

Below:
Small fragments of bread have been placed in the 'hands' of this cut-out, so that it could appear to be taking food from the bird-table. The tomograph is mounted on a jointed rod in such a way that the vertical rod is invisible behind the foliage.

All vegetation was clipped to horizontal and vertical bars. The background, also containing roughly sketched foliage, consists of a large painted board.

120

Above:

Very different effects can be achieved by changing the lighting.

In the first photograph very soft shadows are made by 'bouncing' the lighting indirectly from the white walls of the studio. Unfortunately this procedure tends to bias in favour of yellow. A spotlight illuminates a graded grey back-drop visible through the doorway.

In the second shot the spotlight is off. Direct lighting from one lamp has given hard shadows and a more faithful colour balance.

Fragments of bark, moss etc. were built up on a work-bench to produce this set-up. In the first photograph two spotlights have been used, one to give a graded tone to the back-drop, the other to focus light on the central subject.

In the second shot more general bounced lighting has been used as well as spots. Note how the same back-drop has become a much greyer blue.

and floods to highlight particular areas. Spots may even be coloured in order to strengthen the colour of the background.

Generally speaking direct lighting seems to give the best results, especially if shadows in the 'real' part of the shot accurately correspond to the painted image and to any cast shade or highlights it may contain.

An indirect or 'bounced' light can on the other hand lend a pleasantly flat softness to the picture, and I often simply turn my lights away so that they reflect off the white walls of the studio. Another way is to use white boards or cloths, which can be placed wherever they have the best effect. Indirect lighting of this sort is disadvantageous only in that it tends to make the overall colour more yellow — less blue.

So many tricks are possible — using both traditional and modern equipment — that anyone who knows anything about photography will probably have already thought of dozens of ways in which the image may be improved. I shall mention a few I have tried, full aware of many others I never got round to.

Double or multiple exposures for example, enable the same cut-out(s) to appear in the same picture more than once, perhaps in different postures — wings moved, wheels rotated etc..

To make a double exposure the sheet of film is exposed in two halves by covering opposite halves of the lens for each exposure. A special attachment can be bought for this, but a piece of card will do the job just as well. In between the two exposures, the set-up can be changed, the cut-out altered etc. — just so long as the camera is not moved.

An interesting 'playing card' effect can however be achieved by turning the dark-slide housing completely upside down between the two halves of a double exposure. Adjustments can then be made to the lighting so that the lower half is in shade and does indeed appear to be part of the same set-up.

An adjustable cut-out may be photographed repeatedly against a black back-drop, then finally perhaps with additional scenery, to give the impression that a whole group of individuals is seen. The only disadvantage here of course is that the first cut-out to be exposed inevitably tends to be considerably paler than the last. Overlaps should perhaps be avoided, but in the right circumstances they may produce an interesting effect of transparency.

It is possible to simulate movement by splitting up one long time exposure into a series of short ones. Between each exposure the relevant part — a limb perhaps — is moved slightly, and each exposure is made slightly longer than the

Above:
In this multiple exposure the three distant figures were first photographed as three separate shots against a black background. Between each shot the position of the wings was slightly altered.

Only in the last shot was the foreground foliage included.

The wings are made from painted acetate mounted on copper wire.

Below:
Using a double-exposure attachment, the same subject may be photographed twice in the same image. In this case the camera back was also inverted between the shots and the studio lighting modified.

The symmetry of the background betrays the double exposure, and the change in the blue bias indicates the change in the lighting.

Foreground elements were stuck to the glass screen with double-sided tape.

A black screen was used to eliminate reflections.

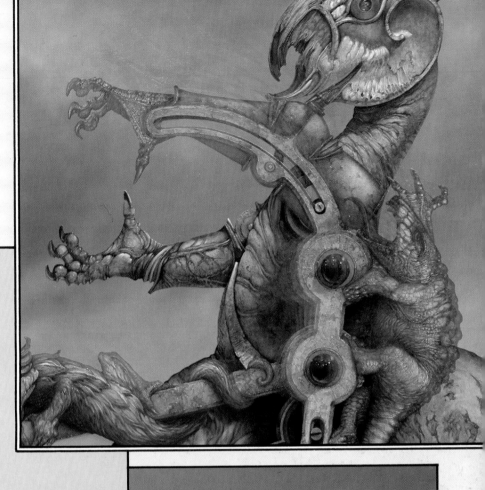

Right:

Several exposures of increasing length appear to give movement to this strange mechanical beast. This tomograph consists of various pivoted and jointed elements turned by wheels.

Glass beads have been used as embellishments, though the beast's eye is only painted.

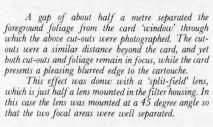

A gap of about half a metre separated the foreground foliage from the card 'window' through which the above cut-outs were photographed. The cut-outs were a similar distance beyond the card, and yet both cut-outs and foliage remain in focus, while the card presents a pleasing blurred edge to the cartouche.

This effect was donw with a 'split-field' lens, which is just half a lens mounted in the filter housing. In this case the lens was mounted at a 45 degree angle so that the two focal areas were well separated.

123

preceding one, until the last — the longest of all — establishes the major part of the image.

The use of various filters can produce all kinds of effects. Particularly effective to represent sparkling stars and beams of light is a star filter. These are available in various patterns, but I have had best results with an eight-point. It must be borne in mind however that the use of a filter always tends to diminish the contrast, and should only be considered when increased atmospherics will not detract from the image.

Another useful gadget is a split-field, which in fact consists only of a simple lens cut in half. This is a most difficult technique, as focussing is very tricky, but it can be very effective where two cut-outs of very different sizes need to appear of similar size. It can focus sharply on two scenes which are physically quite far apart, though there is always a blurred border-line between the two halves of the image, and care must be taken to disguise this by keeping relevant details out of the area.

There are of course dozens of other filters and gadgets on the market — spot filters, graded tones etc., — but as I said earlier, it is quite often the simplest set-up and equipment that produce the most successful image.

The important thing is to design the tomograph in such a way that you know from the very first how it will be used, though obviously it is not always possible to do this. The occasional unexpected success may come from some totally unplanned interaction — the blossoming of a particularly appropriate flower, the chance discovery of some particularly interesting piece of rock, bark etc. — but usually the best image comes with careful forethought. A cut-out creature can be designed to look as though it is perching, hanging from a branch or about to gobble something up; in these cases the very pose of the unreal cut-out demands some interaction with the real props provided for it.

Some of my most effective tricks have been discovered purely by chance. Only when some flowers began to wilt on the set-up did I hit on the idea of simulating a high wind by shooting the whole thing sideways. Flags that appear to flutter in the wind, sea-pinks blustered on the cliff-edge — all are held in place by gravity rather than by the gales. Similarly, wilting vegetation can be made to look quite vigorous by shooting the whole subject upside down.

Whatever the method, the tomograph must be made to appear part of its setting, and although this can be helped by adding appropriate extra touches — by sticking bits of vegetation to the cut-out, by applying droplets of water to a fish's fins or

In the first shot (above) the cut-out was mounted on a rod fixed through my T-shirt to my belt, and in the second (below) the same cut-out was fixed to a glass screen.

Interaction with tomographs is not often successful. The problem seems to be one of movement, blur etc.

A dead mermaid found on the beach.
This is in fact another studio shot. Drops of water
were added with a syringe, though it is sometimes
difficult to tell which are real and which are painted.

Correct positioning of light-sources is essential if
shade and cast shadows are to match up with the way the
tomograph is shaded.

fragments of food to the beak of a bird — the strange truth is that such things do not necessarily make things easier or more effective. A well-painted eye for example, can be just as convincing as a glass one. A painted drop of water stays where you want it and does not dry up under the lights. A painted flower does not wilt.

The photographer — and for that matter the painter too — must always be aware of the fact that his eventual image can be only two-dimensional after all. There is no parallax. One eye is a good as two. So I never assess the effectiveness of any cut-out or set-up with both eyes open. I close one eye, or — better still — look at it through the camera lens.

The technique is interesting but limited. Today I should only consider producing an image by this tomograph method if I were sure it could not possibly be achieved in the conventional way — in other words, only when the painted, unreal elements must necessarily interact with something obviously real or alive.

Aesthetics must also be a consideration. I have found from my experience that the result is rarely a satisfactory substitute for a conventional two-dimensional painting. It is an interesting novelty, but I think it is unlikely to produce anything of great beauty, simply because it is neither reality nor illusion, neither fact nor fiction. The eye and brain cannot help being wary of it, forever looking for the 'join', the trick — instead of reacting to the image itself.

There is also another factor. The relationship between the artist and the viewer, between the writer and the reader, is an unwritten, but nonetheless strict contract. The story-teller says, 'Look, I'll show you my dreams — it's a lot of lies, but never mind.' The listener takes his side, he opts to make a credibility leap, a suspension of disbelief. But if the artist should break that contract, if he tries to deceive — if parts of the lie seem true and parts of the truth lies — then the observer is likely to walk off in disgust. We don't like being tricked — at least not in art. We like to know where the truth begins and the fiction ends.

It is a debatable point whether the tomograph technique can produce anything not more effectively achieved by conventional painting methods.

However, as shown here, it is always a more effective procedure if the cut-out can be designed for a very specific location. In this case the cut-out has a hole through the feet which slots exactly over the perch. No other fixing is needed, and a single lamp provides a realistic raking cast shadow.

THE END